HARI

HILL

FUN BOOK

BOOKS

AVALON

First published in 1999 by Channel 4 Books, an imprint of Macmillan Publishers Ltd,
25 Eccleston Place, London SW1W 9NF, Basingstoke and Oxford.

www.macmillan.co.uk

Associated companies throughout the world.

ISBN 0 7522 1782 8

Text © Harry Hill 1999

A CIP catalogue record for this book is available from the British Library.

Harry Hill Funbook by Harry Hill with additional material by Magda Archer.
Design by the Attic Graphic Design Company Ltd.
Photography by Tessa Hallmann and Chris Frazer Smith.
Costume Design by Leah Archer.
Cover illustration by Magda Archer.

Illustrations:
Harry Hill: Pages 13 *top centre*, 14 top, 36 *bottom left*, 67-68, & 87 *top*
Magda Archer: Pages 7, 9 *top left*, 10 *bottom right*, 15, 17-18, 21-22, 35, 58 *top right*, 59-60, 78, 82
Nick Spender of Advocate: Pages 54-56
Justine Kilburn: Pages 39-40
All other design and illustration by the Attic Graphic Design Company Ltd except this double page spread: by the Attic Graphic Design Company Ltd with special thanks to Magda Archer.
Granada Picture Publicity: Page 76 *frames 23 & 28*
Rex Features Ltd Picture Library: Pages 25 *bottom right*, 46 *top left and right*, 47, 48 *bottom left and top right*, 53, 57, 63, 64 *top left and right*, 71 *top, middle and bottom left*, 87 *bottom left* & 88 *centre left and right*
Typeset by the Attic Graphic Design Company Ltd.
Colour reproduction by Media Junction.
Printed and bound in Italy by New Interlitho, Spa, Milan.

This book
belongs
to ....

....

....

Barrie Gosney
Flat 4, The Albany,
Piccadilly,
London WC1

Hi, I'm Barrie Gosney!

I've been asked by Harry Hill, via my agent, Vanessa Feltz to introduce this book to you. Although as I write I've not seen any book.
Was there supposed to be one, Vanessa? I should get one shouldn't
I? I got the rest of the blurb - "big collar" ...Post modern and
blah blah blah - but no book. Perhaps you could sort it out and get
them to pop one in the post or something. What does he want me to
say? I've only met him a couple of times, who is he? Look, get me
out of it Van, could you?

Yours Barrie

Barrie
x x

P.S. Have you seen my coat? I had it on Saturday night but haven't
seen it since. The grey one.

HARRY HILL BATHTIME IMPRESSIONS

Neat bubble bath, when combined with running water makes, heaps of fluffy white bubbles or "Foam". Why not use the foam for fun with some of my bathtime impressions.

The Big 'Chin' Jimmy Hill

Mr Sgt. Pepper – Peter Blake

A Touch of Frost's David Jason

No Stranger – Acker Bilk

60's Icon Jimi Hendrix

T.V. Funnyman Barry Cryer

The Animal's Friend Rolf Harris

BRAIN THOUGHTS OF
HARRY HILL

People say Barbara Cartland isn't nice looking, but I bet when you see her freshly showered, a little wet gel in her hair, in a light cotton robe - that's when you appreciate her.

Phone up a Pizza delivery place and say, "Have you got any of those pizza balls?" "Pizza balls?" "Yes, you know, when they get all the pizza base and topping and mush it all together into a ball - pizza balls, everyone's doing them." "Well I'm sorry, no we don't do pizza balls." "Oh, goodbye." The thing is, if you phone up enough places, they'll start doing them. Congratulations, you just invented a meal.

I find a good ice breaker at a party is "You look tired!"

At the end of the war things are pretty messy and confused. That's when you move in and steal a couple of pads of paper, some pens - stationery equipment. Of course everything should be accounted for, but in a long war like the Second World War - who's going to miss a few stationery items. Don't get caught, don't mention my name because after wars you can get shot for that sort of thing.

If you're on death row go quietly to the execution chamber then, as they go to strap you in the chair, struggle a lot and start crying - it might just work.

If your girlfriend wants to dump you, just avoid all her calls and don't open any of her letters, that way she can't say she's dumped you and technically you're still going out.
Ha ha you've won!

If they ever introduce the Hindu Caste system in Britain, try and get put down as a Brahmin because they have it slightly easier. If you get assessed as a pariah, appeal.

It's a bit disconcerting when you're explaining your problem to the doctor and you look over and in your notes he's just drawing a big lady's bra.

Wow!
Look at the size of those hawthorn berries! Tomatoes sorry.

Scientists think they got the answer with DNA, well wait till they hear about this new thing I've discovered - PNA. It's like DNA only this time you don't have to gather it - it's just there!

Tap Dancing:
What are you trying to say exactly?

I suppose a modern Totem Pole would include likenesses of film stars, inventors - Tom Cruise, Jack Nicholson, and wait, whose face is that I see peering from the top - my little friend Jonty. How the hell did he get up there?

I hate it after a restaurant meal when people quibble over the bill. "I had that." "I didn't have that." That's why I insist on diners keeping a tally as they go along. Don't make a big thing of it. Some small pads and pencils each and a calculator in the middle of the table.

Isn't it annoying when you get so attached to your hostages you almost kind of don't want the ransom to be paid.

Did Jesus ride on a donkey? Yes, but knowing him he probably didn't have an ice cream.

I would never do full frontal nudity even if the script required it. Although I suppose if they increased the money, yes I would do it. Even if the script required it or not.

He felt the "rush" come over him as he stood on the train in rush hour.

Search your soul by all means but maybe it got mixed up with those papers you threw out?

Is it me or is Cluedo the same people hanging round the same house waiting to get murdered?

4

BE GARY FOR A DAY

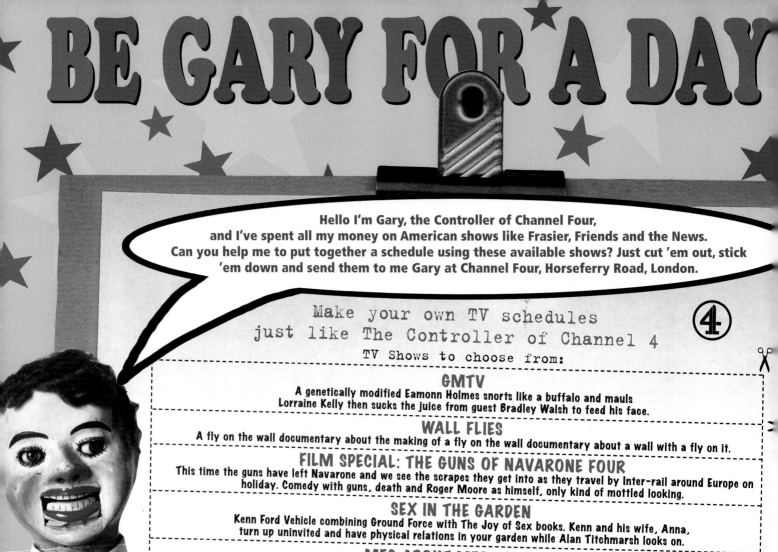

Hello I'm Gary, the Controller of Channel Four,
and I've spent all my money on American shows like Frasier, Friends and the News.
Can you help me to put together a schedule using these available shows? Just cut 'em out, stick
'em down and send them to me Gary at Channel Four, Horseferry Road, London.

Make your own TV schedules
just like The Controller of Channel 4
TV Shows to choose from:

GMTV
A genetically modified Eamonn Holmes snorts like a buffalo and mauls
Lorraine Kelly then sucks the juice from guest Bradley Walsh to feed his face.

WALL FLIES
A fly on the wall documentary about the making of a fly on the wall documentary about a wall with a fly on it.

FILM SPECIAL: THE GUNS OF NAVARONE FOUR
This time the guns have left Navarone and we see the scrapes they get into as they travel by Inter-rail around Europe on
holiday. Comedy with guns, death and Roger Moore as himself, only kind of mottled looking.

SEX IN THE GARDEN
Kenn Ford Vehicle combining Ground Force with The Joy of Sex books. Kenn and his wife, Anna,
turn up uninvited and have physical relations in your garden while Alan Titchmarsh looks on.

MEG ABOUT MEG, TO MEG
Meg Ryan talks to Mystic Meg about Meg Richardson from 70's soap "Crossroads". Also with Goldie Hawn.

EURO BARREL
We scrape the bottom of the barrel and see what is left. Very adult, very now, more please.

FILM: THE GUNS OF NAVARONE FIVE
In this sequel to The Guns of Navarone 4 the Guns of Navarone, now based in New York,
fall in love with Meg Ryan then discover that one of the guns is firing blanks.
Moving Romantic Love story with guns, impotence and Meg Ryan or Goldie Hawn.

PARKINSON
Cecil Parkinson tells us about how to be naughty and get away with it.
Week One "eradicating your smell". How to leave no trace in a lady's boudoir.

FILM '86
with Barry Norman (repeat)

KEATS, KEATING, KEATON AND COTTON
Poetry, Gloria Hunniford's daughter, silent comedy and Dot from Eastenders
all together in one show. No preview tapes available.

NEVER MIND THE BALLCOCKS
Plumbing Trivia Quiz with Phil Jupitus, in a basement filling up with water
and he's got three lengths of copper down pipe and only two washers to fix it.

WHICH ONE'S ON STEROIDS THEN?
Sports quiz in which a celebrity panel feel up sports stars for the
side effects of steroids and then get urine tests back.

BEAN THERE, DUNN THAT
Clive Dunn and Christopher Beany talk about their lives in showbizniss.

PRO CELEBRITY SILD FIGHTS
Britain's most popular oily fish joins forces with such stars
as Goldie Hawn and Christopher Beany and they wack out the truth with fish.

CAN'T COOK REPORT, WON'T COOK REPORT
Roger Cook shows how much food he has eaten over the years
from his fascinating food diaries. Episode One: Meat.

CHANNEL 4

Time	
6.00am	
6.55	
9.00	
9.25	
11.15	
12.05pm	
12.30	
2.25	
4.00	
6.00	
6.30	
7.00	
8.00	
9.00	
10.00	
12.05am	
12.35	

INSER
YOUR C
PICK OF T
PIC H

Cut and paste your schedule here

6

Barrie Gosney
Flat 4, The Albany,
Piccadilly,
London WC1

TO:
Greg Bacon
14 The Strand
London WC1

Dear Greg,

You haven't seen my coat have you? The grey one, yes I had it on
Saturday night at the club, well I think I had it. Do you remember seeing me in my grey coat on Saturday Greg? With the patch
pockets? Do you think you could let me know whether you think you
saw me in my coat on Saturday?

All the best,

Barrie

Barrie

P.S. My gloves are in the pockets.

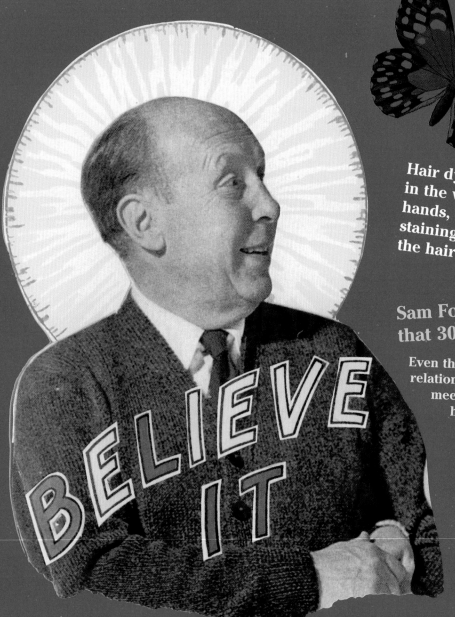

BELIEVE IT

The Cabbage White butterfly is a fly but is not made from either cabbage or butter. The fact that hot cabbage benefits from a knob of butter is mere crazy happenstance.

Hair dye, in the wrong hands, can cause staining of the skin around the hair and also your towel.

Sam Fox, in recent DNA tests, shows that 30% of her body hair is inhaled.

Even though you and your mortgage have a close relationship for over twenty years you will never meet. English law demands that because your home may be at risk if you do not keep up the mortgage repayments on your house you may never meet your mortgage for, if you were to fall in love and want to marry, the mortgage may choose to waive some of the payments putting the building society out of pocket.

Jean Shrimpton eats a ton of shrimp every year.

Suede shoes were originally made by a cobbler in the seventeenth century as a joke but caught on and were later adopted by rock group Madness as their shoe of choice.

Actors are so suspicious they hate to hear the word "Macbeth" during a production. Other words they don't like are "Flop" and "It stinks".

Midgets think that tree trunks are wooden storage canisters for height.

In the Demi Moore vehicle "Ghost" the pot she made in the famous potter's wheel scene was fired and glazed and now contains the ghost star of the film.

We only bend our legs to take up the excess slack that occurs in them when we walk.

Stonehenge is in fact the top of a much larger submerged structure for finger knitting by the dinosaur/giants.

If you cross a kangaroo with a sheep you do not get a woolly jumper but a hybrid that is neither accepted by the sheep or kangaroo populations and destined to die out within one generation.

Venetian blinds do not come from Venus, they are a franchise.

Circuses were originally places where animals could meet for illicit interbreeding of species. The term "Big Top" means literally "Tented overcovering for illicit interspecies breeding."

Fly spray is also known in some houses as "Window White Patch Causer" because of its propensity, when sprayed at a fly at close range abutting up to / close to a window, of causing "White-Patch".

Babies have antlers which are absorbed in the womb a crazy one week before birth.

Bobby Charlton is not, in fact, related to Jack Charlton. The name is coincidence and Jack spent a one-million-dollar fortune in plastic surgery and voice coaching to join the exclusive Charlton Clan.

Puppets are often tiny representations of real people.

The original design for cassette tapes made them the size of attache cases. Marketing was delayed for fifteen years while scientists worked round the clock on a smaller format.

Superstitious supermarket chain Sainsburys always include a sweep in their board meetings as they believe it will bring them luck.

Adolph Hitler would never stand to urinate but preferred to sit down to do it like a lady.

Nutty comic Bradley Walsh's real name is Reynaud Bradfox meaning literally Fox Brad Fox.

OR NEIGH!

Actor Martin Shaw, when making cult ITV show "The Professionals" was not told it was a cop show. Right up until the first screenings he believed it was a show about the different acoustics you get in disused warehouses.

Barry Manilow cannot in fact sing "Many-low" notes and according to Amish law should be re-christened Barry "Broad spread of".

Furniture vans go through long periods when they contain absolutely no furniture whatsoever.

Although we consider the octopus to have eight legs the octopus itself only considers two of them legs and terms the other "Repeats".

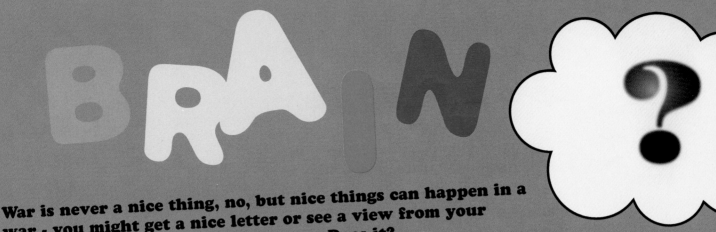

BRAIN ?

War is never a nice thing, no, but nice things can happen in a war - you might get a nice letter or see a view from your barracks but that doesn't justify war. Does it?

You know at Christmas? What is the religious significance of a silver pine cone?

I wouldn't ever want to be in a situation where they had to liquefy my food. I'd rather take my chances with more solid food thanks.

What protection does Welsh national dress offer against dragons?

You can recognise people by their walk but a much easier way is their face. And if you're still not sure call their name "Andy" and if he turns round it's him.

Chaos theory says that if a butterfly flaps its wings in Bangkok it causes a hurricane in Miami. So correct me if I'm wrong but what they're saying is kill all the butterflies, right?

People don't seem to take any notice of fog warnings. Maybe they would if it was renamed death gas. Same with rain - rename it crash liquid; snow - pile-up inducement flakes and sunshine - safety powder.

A rattle is a plaything for a baby but a rattlesnake is a venomous reptile found in the desert - the clue is in the "SNAKE" bit.

Do you ever get the skins off your baked beans and wear them as protective teeth?

Here's a tough one for you: jigsaw puzzle of a mosaic.

How about a cream cracker that doesn't break when you butter it? Don't make them chewy though - yuk!

I think the message from ITV's "Birds of a Feather", if there is one, is that two ladies living together, husbands in prison, with a nosy female neighbour, get into a lot of hilarious situations.

In the film "The Usual Suspects" it would be good to have a bit at the end where they just explain the whole thing out really clearly. Was Kaiser Sosay involved or not. Oh and in the film "Speed" why does the coach have to go so fast - slow down.

There's pancake day so why not a popcorn day?

Freeze-dried coffee. Where do you keep it, in the freezer or the dryer?

BIG

THOUGHTS

Is stubble new hairs or old hairs with the top cut off?

Shouldn't ground to air missiles be called ground to air to ground again missiles?

Is there such a thing as a just war? I don't know but you'd find it next to the "Just William" books in the library.

They say "frightened rabbit" in the road. Frightened or "brave"?

They say we humans are 98% water so who's got the other 2%?

I heard that the queen wasn't that bothered about who won the Second World War just so long as it stops soon please.

I suppose a STOP! sign to a church organist means two different things but it still don't mean GO so blow in the bag please Mr Organist.

How come when I copy it's plagiarism yet someone else copies it's research?

If I ran a bed and breakfast I wouldn't have tea and coffee making facilities in the rooms because what's wrong with my tea and coffee?

If Jesus was a carpenter let's hope his teachings are better than his carpentry because none of his carpentry has survived.

We've got a dishwasher but how about such a thing as a machine that picks up the dirty dishes from your table and puts them in the dishwasher - a dish harvester it is called. But careful, don't leave any clean dishes out or it'll have them... or any pets... or young children. Look out! It's the dish harvester! I guess the dish harvester is a sort of allegory for death.

Churchill was a great leader and Church Hill is a great slider when covered in snow and ice. Are they related? Who cares?

Should ladies wear fur coats? Well, maybe another way of looking at it is not so much fur as "furry leather".

OF

ALA

12

SCURF™

What is SCURF™?
SCURF™ is a disease popular amongst today's teenagers. What happens is, due to their debauched Ibiza / Manumission / Rave / Lara Croft / Prodigy / Hooch lifestyle of ready meals and mind expanding (shrinking, more like!) drug culture God has delivered SCURF™ on them to make us think twice.

How do I know if I've got SCURF™?
SCURF™ takes the form of tiny scalp nodules or Scurfules that expand, burst and release their spores onto the shoulders of your sports-wear/hooded sweater things that you all seem to wear these days.

What does SCURF™ look like under the microscope?
If we look at a SCURF™ nugget under the electron microscope we see a basic boil down of all the bad habits that you've got into with your ready meals / docusoap / tabloid exposé / entrapment / girl in hotel / boy band / shoot 'em up / shoes that you pump up with air / nose ring / wonder bra / perfume advert sniff sniff Marie Claire / millennium bug / unleaded / Ground Force / Changing Rooms / The Adelphi / Frasier / mentality of modern life.

How do I stop SCURF™?
You can't stop SCURF™! You think you can get rid of SCURF™ by just turning up to confession like a Catholic? You really think it's as simple as that, you loser? You got SCURF™ because of your life of sleaze and DIY programmes and make-overs. Your scalp is a mess as it pays for your lifestyle errors and you are forced to bear the visible stigmata of SCURF™.

SCURF VICTIM

- sparse hair pushed out of the way by scurf.™
- mind full of muck
- Tears of regret well, it's too late for booze buster
- Scurf™ nodules
- Piercings
- Scarf Spores
- combing ain't gonna help you now
- no need for a mirror you loser
- Low pockets full of scurf
- long gusset
- weird shoes that you puff up with air.

" Small boys still thrust their hands into the pockets of their first trousers."

Gregory Bacon
14 The Strand
London WC1

To Barrie Gosney
Flat 4 The Albany
Piccadilly

Dear Barrie,
Thank you for your letter and sorry to hear about your coat. I think I did see you in your coat on saturday, yes, but can't be a hundred per cent on it. Have you phoned the club to see whether the coat's been handed in? Awfully annoying when you lose a coat and that green one was awfully smart, it would be a shame to lose it.
Best of luck with the coat business

Gregory Bacon

Greg

" A piece of imaginary beefsteak for dinner."

13

Fortune Teller Fish

Place Fish in the palm of the hand and its movements
will indicate

Moving Head . . . . Jealousy
Moving Tail . . . . Indifference
Moving Head and Tail . . . . . . Cloying, irritating personality
Curling Sides . . . . False deceitful arrogant swine
Motionless . . . . Aggressive twerp
Curls up Entirely . . . . Central heating too high
Turns Over . . . . The fish never done that afore,
Call the elders!
To the duckin' stool!

MADE IN JAPAN △

Barrie Gosney
Flat 4 The Albany
Piccadilly,
London WC1

To The Doorman
The Carlton Club
Piccadilly
London WC1

Dear Bootsie,
Listen, you haven't had a coat handed in have you? You know my
grey top coat? Well I've lost it and my gloves and lord knows
what else are in the pockets. I can't be certain I was wearing
the coat but I can't think where else it might have got to.
Perhaps you could check the security footage to see if I'm
wearing my coat saturday last but one. Am I wearing the coat?
In the meantime I'll make my own enquiries.
Your help is much appreciated.
Yours faithfully

Barrie
x x
Barrie Gosney

Barrie Gosney
Flat 4 The Albany
Piccadilly,
London WC1

To Gregory Bacon
14 The Strand
London WC1

Dear Greg,
Thank you for your letter in response to my letter
regarding the temporary (I hope any rate) mislaying of my
coat. You mention a green coat. I haven't got a green
coat, it was a grey coat that I have lost and was asking
whether you can remember me wearing it saturday last but
one. Who's this person in a green coat? Please think back
Greg. Its important, my gloves were in that coat.

All the best

Barrie
x x
Barrie

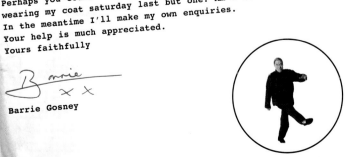

14

Harry's Favourite Dinners

Menu

Monday
Starter:
Fruit juice
Main:
Cold cuts from Sunday's roast, mash and peas
Sweet:
Cold apple pie and custard / or yoghurt

Tuesday
Starter:
Prawn cocktail
Main:
Giant sausage roll
Sweet:
Yoghurt

Wednesday
Starter:
Tomato juice
Main:
Lamb curry with sultanas and side order of dessicated coconut
(for sprinkling on top like they do in India)
Sweet:
Chocolate instant whip and evap.

Thursday
Starter:
Melon
Main:
"Toad"
Sweet:
Jelly with dream topping

Friday
Starter:
Campbell's cream of tomato soup
Main:
2 chops (pork or lamb), 2 scoops of mash
Sweet:
Fruit cocktail with Tip-Top

Saturday
Starter:
Ritz crackers and Primula
Main:
Sandwich selection
Sweet:
Butterscotch Angel Delight

Sunday
Starter:
Grapefruit with glacé cherry garnish (in middle)
Main:
Individual Birds Eye roast platter (or Iceland's own brand) with trimmings
Extra gravy from granules if needed
Sweet:
Tinned prunes and custard

Note : Feast days - Easter, Christmas day. Large Capon with all the trimmings!

BRIGHTON
PIER
RIDE TICKET

172571

"Here's Health"

COUGH
MIXTURE

NEW

ALMOST AS NICE AS TH

Paint by Numbers

1 DARK BLUE   3 YELLOW   5 FLESH
2 LIGHT BLUE   4 RED   6 BROWN

Burt's Page

Hey! Harry! This book stinks!

Its Burt Kwouk!

Hey readers! Wanna catch a chicken? I've identified three foolproof methods each demonstrating a higher level of commitment.

1) Dangle a line off the flats with a single piece of corn at the end and just wait for mister chicken to bite. (Initial outlay cost: 1 tin of corn 34p, 1 bamboo cane 12p, 1 piece of string 80p : Grand total £1.26: Return - One chicken.)

2) Contaminate the chicken farm's water supply with iron filings, then drive by the farm with one of those electro magnets like you see in scrap yards. (Initial outlay cost: £13.50 for iron filings, £246 for plant hire, but you may catch 300 to 400 chickens in one scoop.)

3) Genetically modify the DNA of a bird you already own and cross breed that with a friend's bird. (Start up costs: Outbuildings to convert to lab £12,000, DNA separation equipment £60,000, Staff wage bill £80,000 - including poaching finest scientific minds from abroad, Post-It notes for labelling samples 72p, Incubators £25,000, PR consultant to put positive spin on initial disastrous experiment results @£40 an hour. Total cost in excess of £200,000 but has the advantage of being able to supply many thousands of chickens.)

These are the methods, each with their own limitations, and like any procedure you must weigh up start costs against potential rewards and if that doesn't help then do my Chicken Catching Dance - it won't help you catch a chicken but it'll distract your creditors and keep the heat off for another week!

```
HEY LITTLE HEN
WHEN WHEN WHEN
WILL YOU LAY ME AN EGG FOR MY TEA
HEY LITTLE HEN
WHEN WHEN WHEN
WILL YOU TRY TO SUPPLY ONE FOR ME.
```

Burt Kwouk there!

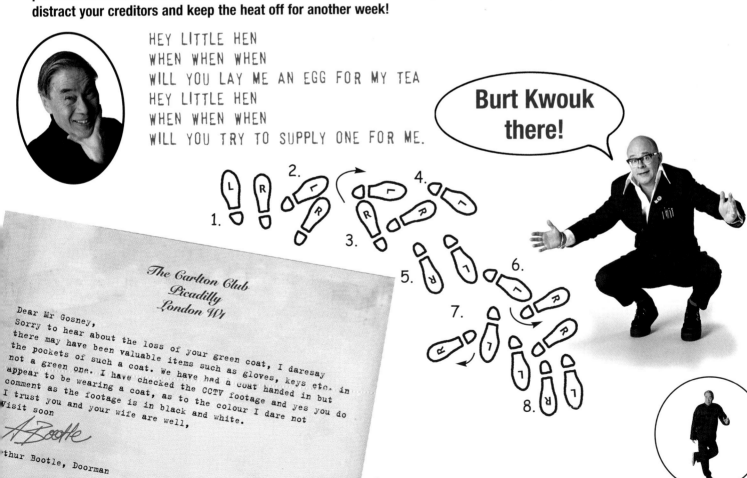

The Carlton Club, Picadilly, London W1

Dear Mr Gosney,

Sorry to hear about the loss of your green coat, I daresay there may have been valuable items such as gloves, keys etc. in the pockets of such a coat. We have had a coat handed in but not a green one. I have checked the CCTV footage and yes you do appear to be wearing a coat, as to the colour I dare not comment as the footage is in black and white. I trust you and your wife are well. Visit soon

Arthur Bootle, Doorman

NATURE

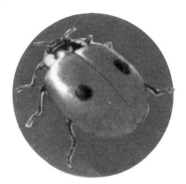

THE LADYBIRD
Red and black
It wears a sort of mac
It flies around
homeward
bound until it
lands on my
finger.
Hello Mrs Ladybird
Haven't you heard
The well known rhyme
about you?

THE HORSE
The horse, the horse
Of course
The horse
Is a favourite of
The Queen
He's brown or grey
Palamino or bay
I wish I had one.

THE CROW
Bold and ugly
Is the crow.

THE HAMSTER
The hamster is
A-wheel
He knows not
what
time of day
it is.
Oh, Hammie can
I tempt thee with
a sunflower seed?

THE MOUSE
You're so small
Mr Mouse or
MM for short and yes, you
are short until
you get caught and then I
wouldn't
like to be in
your shoes.

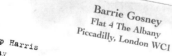

Barrie Gosney
Flat 4 The Albany
Piccadilly, London WC1

To Phillip Harris
14 Kingsway
London WC1

Dear Phil,
Barrie Gosney here, sorry to bother you but can you remember what
the weather was like last Saturday but one? You see I've lost my
coat and suspect I left it at the Club. I'm not certain though. If
I knew the weather was wet on that night (Saturday last) then I
would almost certainly have worn the coat. If however it was mild
then I might very well have worn my suit jacket and taken the pack
a mac as a precaution. You're always pretty good with the old
memory box Phil, was it fine that night (saturday last but one) or
as I'm hoping, wet?
Yours expectantly

Barrie
x x
Barrie
PS Was I wearing the coat? Do you remember that fact? Or had I
left it with the attendant prior to joining you
and Greg.
CC. Greg Bacon

TABLE

THE TORTOISE
So slow
Are you on a
go slow?
You are hardly
Seb Coe.
You're slow
and certainly
no
Mr T.

THE PUPPY
So cute the
Pup
running
around with my cup.

THE CAT
My friend the cat
lies on
the mat
waiting for me
to feed her
Miaow says she
and then we
know she
needs feeding.

THE CANARY
Canary
you are
fairly
small
Fly around the
Room while you've
got the
Chance.

Hilarious Dog Stories
by L. M. Hand
No.1 Annie Does Her Business

One day Annie, my two-year-old *Fox Terrier bitch*, and I were playing "fetch-me-the-ball" in the local park - larking around, chasing squirrels, getting to know Pippin - the new *Cocker* on the block, stealing Misty's new rag bone... Misty, I might add is a three-year-old *Golden*... when all of a sudden a dog fight began - and by "dog fight" I mean in the medieval sense! Well, before we knew it Tosh - the *Irish*, was throwing his weight around and Lady had joined the scuffle! Somehow someone managed to break the fight up but in the meantime a most preposterous smell had arrived. Well, do you know what had happened? In the heat of the moment my young *Terrier* had done her business! Golly how we laughed!

THE RABBIT
Everyone loves
the dear old
Bunny
Floppy ears and nose so
runny - has she
had her
injections?

Barrie Gosney
Flat 4 The Albany
Piccadilly, London WC1

Round Robin to all members of Carlton Club.

Dear Friends,

We have all at one time or another lost something or someone dear to us. Has anyone seen my coat?You probably all remember my grey Top coat. Patch pockets, Epaulets, pretty standard. I have lost the coat and the contents of the coat pockets of which I can only be sure of the gloves.
Could you let me know if you have any knowledge of the whereabouts of the coat at the above address?
Also has anyone seen the gloves - brown dents, fleece lined?
All information about the coat or gloves would be gratefully received and treated in the strictest of confidence.

Yours

Barrie Gosney

My Day by Stouffer

7.00am

Wake up and wave off my current girlfriend - Anne Diamond. Anne has been coming round ever since the break with Mike and her and her sons often stay over too. Anne brings me a moist kipper in bed and a bowl of tea before showering down and kissing me goodbye. She's a nice girl and makes a mean banana parfait.

7.30am

Regurgitate kippers and re-eat them. I dunno why I do this but I got into the habit of eating then re-eating about two years ago when I started going to Glenn Hoddle's psychic.

7.45am

Adam Ricketts (Nick Tilsley from 'Corrie') comes round and we do our thousand sit-ups each. Sit-ups can be so boring by yourself and I met Adam after my stint on Coronation Street when I stood in for Julie Goodyear during the transition phase to Racquel. We both had an interest in sit-ups and he suggested that he, and his friend Peter Andre come round every morning and compete for cash money. Pete dropped out after the third day claiming "previous commitments" but Adam and I both knew he was scared of the "sit-up factory", as we call it. Adam towels down and joins me in a tin of Banana Slimfast™ before faxing himself to work.

8.00am

John Humphries at the Today™ programme phones and asks for a comment regarding the single European currency. I tell him simply that convergence must be allowed to take place and that we must be patient, John. Off air he thanks me for "a stonking quote" and my ego is inflated to half full but I know I must get more strokings if I am to feel comfortable.

8.30am

Car arrives to pick me up and take me to the GMTV studios for my weekly round up of world conflicts or "Stouffer's Wars - who's Goosin' who" as they call it. I like to make the driver wait to show him who is boss and receive two ego puff points in the process.

9.30am

Car takes me to GMTV. The driver used to run a chain of supermarkets but was made redundant during the eighties and has been forced to drive for a living. I feign sympathy and ask him to place a hand under my Armani chemise and feel my washboard six-pack stomach.

9.50am

Too late to do my GMTV spot. They have got Jimmy Greaves in to do a spot on conflict in general. "Keep it light, Jimmy!" the producer barks. I ask if there is somewhere where I can take my dose of cat nip. I am shown to an ill lit stairwell, littered with syringes, and sniff hard on the muslin bag of nip. Then Eammon Holmes appears. "Any nip going?" he says and takes a deep toke on the bag. His face transforms temporarily into that of a cat's. He purrs gently, then we are snatched from our dreamlike state by Mr Motivator. "Hey guys! Coming down the canteen?"

10.00am

We follow Motivator down the corridors to the canteen where I gorge myself on the special of Sild. Motivator opts for the vegetable ragout and I look at his scalp, laden with Scurf™ and smile to myself.

10.30am

Car to take me to my agent Ivan Pretchikov. As I leave the studio there is a gaggle of middle aged ladies dressed as me - 'The Malfos' as they call themselves, or "Middle Aged Lady Fans of Stouffer". They smother me with kisses and the acrid smell of their scent fills my nostrils. Four ego puff points.

11.00am

Meet up with Ivan at The Groucho. I look across at The Pet Shop Boys who wave and beckon over the waiter. Five minutes later a bottle of sparkling mineral water arrives with a note: "To Stouffer, love you - The Pets". They're nice boys but I wouldn't want my sister to marry one. Ivan talks to me about his new hat that he bought from the latest fancy hat boutique. "You should get one Stouff', they're really happening." We go on to discuss the various corporate entertainments that he has me booked for and the possibility of replacing Carl Howman in the Flash adverts. It would be great to land the lucrative "Flash" deal, that would be a nice piece of meat to put on the ego plate and financially would mean I could cut all ties with the late nite cult comic Harry Hill. Liam Gallagher, Patsy and Roy Walker arrive together - all wearing Ivan's fancy hat, and I make a note to get one. Our meeting over, I sidle over to Roland Rat's table, he's sitting chatting to Bagpus, Orville, Cuddles and Kate Moss and we catch up on all the latest hot gossip. Orville opened 'Orvilles' night club in 1985 after his success with Keith Harris and it has become THE showbusiness haunt of the late nineties. On any one night you might see Viv Westwood, Valentino, Meg Matthews and Richard O'Sullivan.

1.00pm

Lunch with Tony Blair. Blair asked me to help promote his new project - an additional commandment that he has come up with and would like to see adopted by the Christian Church. He tells me it's "Thou shalt tell off the naughty" but I don't go for it. Basically I'm seeing this lunch with Blair as a) A free meal on the tax payer and b) 12 ego puff points. I tell TB he's wasting his time and he bursts into tears threatening to "Sue my ass". I regurgitate my lunch and eat it right in his face.

2.30pm

Ivan calls and tells me Harry Hill has been on the phone. I tell him to stonewall him. "Tell him to bike the scripts round - and they'd better be good, and he'd better have his wallet handy." I purr.

3.15pm

Nap time. I like to curl up in a shop doorway and nap - just to remind myself of my roots and background - that of a humble cat growing up in a slum.

4.00pm

Home. I get all the daily newspapers and spread them out before me. I circle any world conflicts in crayon and digest the information to regurgitate on my GMTV spot.

5.00pm

Prepare for the evening's corporate entertainments slot. I am presenting an award to the Laminates Industry - kitchen work surfaces, that sort of thing. I always ask for a list of the employees and their addresses and arrange for a private detective to follow the key players around for a week, gathering information about them - extra-marital affairs, shady business dealings, visits to massage parlours etc. so I can tailor my presentation to the clients involved.

5.30pm

Ivan phones, I lost the Flash advert to Carl again. I phone Carl to congratulate him - it's O.K. we're friends.

6.00pm

Corporate entertainments slot. A fight breaks out when I reveal that the managing director's wife is sleeping with the head of finance. I leave under a hail of recriminations, making sure that Ivan gets the cheque first.

9.00pm

Present "Best New Hat" award at the Brits. The award goes to Barry Gibb's trilby and Jay Kay is furious. He rips up the seat fur and gorges on it and nearly falls out of the bouncy castle. Jarvis Cocker leaves the soft play area and comes to his aid. Denise weeps into a thermos.

10.00pm

Creep into bed taking care not to wake Anne. I mentally count up the number of ego puff points I have received over the day's shenanigans - fourteen - not bad. The world's conflicts swirl about my head as sleep's sweet healer overtakes me. Ah, it's a cat's life.

(H - Do you think this bit "Ah, it's a cat's life" is too corny? I can take it out if you prefer? - S)

Mum's Rules

MUM RUNS A PRETTY TIGHT SHIP!

MUM SEZ

Wipe down all light switches after use and check three times that switch still working. Wash hands after each switch depression

Flush toilet once after waters, twice after dirties. Hold handle down for 1 minute and wipe after use

Lights out and bedroom door locked 8.30 unless "The Professionals" on TV when can stay up to end

Do not interfere with stun gun recharging module. When red light shows it is recharging

Do not talk while Trevor McDonald is on TV

Washing up to be done directly after meals, clean plates and utensils to each be placed in individual polythene bags and dated with marker pen for hygiene

Socks to be folded together prior to placement in sock drawer

Crow poison to be put down alternate nights and dead crows to be cleared away following morning

Shake SCURF™ nodules from clothes into receptacle provided

Footbath at front door to be topped up with Dettol weekly

Do not pick at sealant around bath, CCTV footage will disclose culprit and stun gun will be employed

No derogatory comments about Peter Sarstedt or his natural successor "Steps"

No sild allowed on the premises

Staves in traps to be sharpened and tested once a month. All traps to be inspected and emptied daily

No girls back, friends must sign non disclosure contract

Nothing must interfere with Mum's bedtime song (Where do you Go to My Lovely... by Peter Sarstedt. (Alternatively Thank Abba for the Music by Steps)

Always wipe seat or put paper down

FAILURE TO OBEY ONE OR MORE OF THESE RULES WILL RESULT IN EMPLOYMENT OF STUN GUN

MY TWELVE fAVOURITE POST-IT NOTES

Please wake me for meals

Please stop feeding the dog charcoal briquettes — he's supposed to smell like that.

MONICA LEWINSKY'S BABY NEEDS A HAIRCUT

HARRY
PLEASE TAPE GUNS OF NAVARONE
—Burt

If NAN PHONES FROM HOME PLEASE MAINTAIN "HITLER HAS WON" CHARADE AND FEIGN GERMAN ACCENT

KURT RUSSELL IS IN THE SPARE ROOM IF THE PHONE RINGS AND IT'S GOLDIE — STONEWALL HER!

MUM'S DEAD

THE BRASS BEAR IN THE HALL IS WARM PLEASE disist from INCESSANT rubbing

you're adopted

Barry Gibb has got Van Morrison's hat and he'd like it back please.

Hostage's relatives phoned Will we do deal for cash?

This way up. yes but which way is up?

If you spill coffee on your cheque book, to remove the stain just wash it with you[r] paying in book.

And now a head stand. Whooaoooooah! Ouch! You were supposed to catch my legs!

Ever on the phone and you start kissing it? Why do we do that?

I think we all dream of one day opening a petting zoo. Small mammals at first, rodents, perhaps some birds but there's a lot of work involved - get foreign students to help out. There would be problems - flu sweeps through the squirrel enclosure - 4 dead, 3 in bed with magazines. Mr Badger's cut his foot on a piece of glass - "Please sweep the badger pen more thoroughly Monique!" Just teething problems and at £4.50 a ticket you're laughing - save up for an otter, a real crowd pleaser, plough the money back into the business. But for the time being Fly Zoo. The star attraction? A bee.

Am I the only person to think that the grey squirrels were just elderly red squirrels?

We were watching a thing about these fancy Calvin Klein pants and my wife turned to me and said "If you ever make it big, you won't go for those fancy pants?" And I promised her that if I ever made it big I would never change my pants.

...laster off it had turned into an arm.

In the future there will be many more older people in our communities. Where will they live? We'll get out in a flat bed truck with a harpoon tagging them. That's how we can find out.

Bad breath? No mate, just different breath.

Take away the elephant's trunk and what have you got? Well, a large grey shire horse, oh and also a severed trunk, oh my god it's bleeding and still moving, look!

UGHTS

HILL

Remember when Clip Frames came in? Wow! Fantastic! You could frame your own pictures at a fraction of the cost of a professional framer. Then you realised you weren't so much framing as pressing the picture between a piece of glass and a piece of hardboard. I thought it was too good to be true.

I think if I had a choice I'd like to come back as a slug because, no, hear me out, not many people would choose a slug and so I could have the pick of them - maybe even king slug. Also if I didn't like my new slug life, slugs don't live long so in a couple of weeks I choose again.

When choosing a good mayor it's important not to choose someone who likes wearing a chain or has a superficial love of the tricorn hat.

Ever do that thing in the school photo where you run round the back and appear twice? If you time it wrong and run too early you don't appear in the first bit and then you arrive late and don't appear in the second bit either and don't appear at all. Of course if the whole school do that the picture comes out blank.

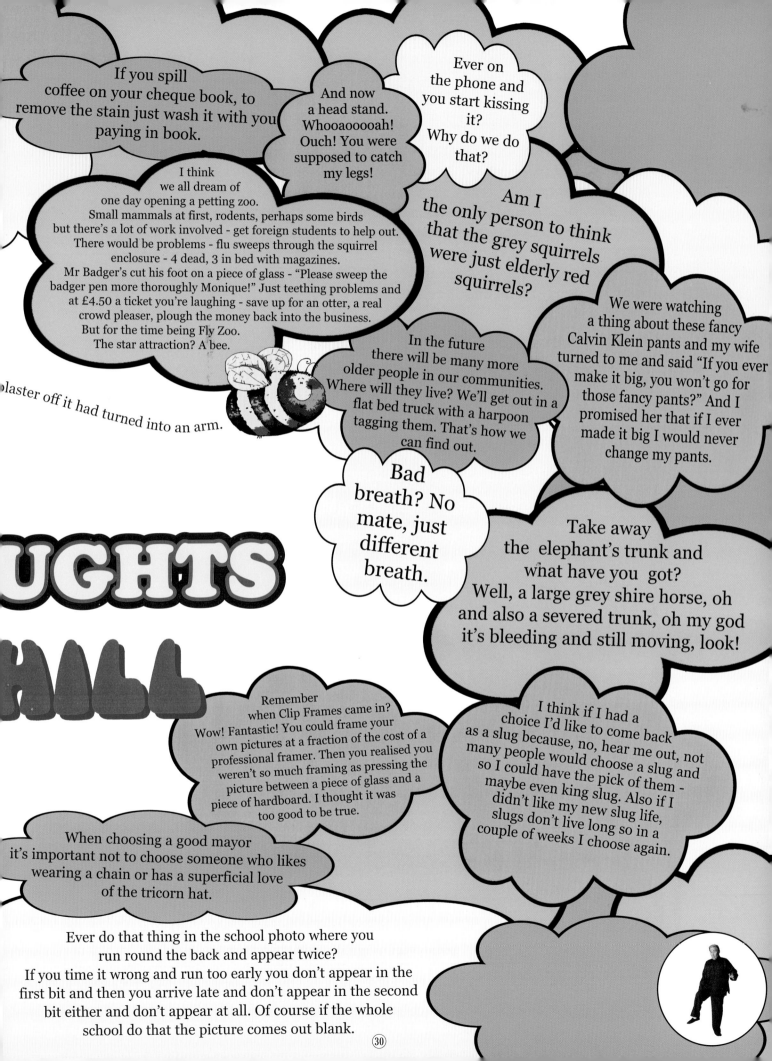

"Join My New Religion"

Says Harry Hill

Thank you for buying this book and buying into a different view of life – what I call "The Notnormals". You may also be interested in taking things a stage further and joining my new religion: The Sacred Church of the Notnormal under the divine guidance of Harry Hill – where Outcasts or Freaks like us can meet unhindered by the artificial restraints imposed by the Internet/New Labour/Ground Force/Docusoap Loving/Crow Fancying Scurfheads.

When I was hard up in the eighties (weren't we all?) I got on the job seekers allowance and started up my own religion.

Harry Hill is a registered religion.

Harry Hill Sacred Church of the Freaks now has its own currency and I would urge you to cash up your British pounds and pence into Harry Hill Dollars by sending it in the envelopes provided.

EVENTS

1. <u>Jumble Sale</u> Staplehurst Village Hall, Kent. Feb 4th 2.30 - 5.30
Bring and buy Jumble to raise money for the refurbishment of the Harry Hill Temple in Marden. Get there early for the bargains before the Gypsies get them.
2. <u>Crow Hunt</u> Feb 21st 11.00am until 4.30 approx.
Followers are invited to assemble in the fourth field with their guns to shoot at Crows. 2 points for every crow, 1 point for a rook. Twelve points gains you an audience with Harry (And I don't mean like in "An audience with Lilly Savage" on LWT) Tickets HH$12.00
3. <u>Sacred Badger Parade and blessing</u> 4.00pm 28th Feb
You are invited to attend the annual badger parade and asked to come dressed in outfits from the hit late nite TV Show "Harry Hill" on Channel 4 which has laid down the rules which now govern our lives. Leading the parade will be the badgers Gareth Southgate Badger, Tasmin Archer Badger and Jools Holland Badger. Then the massed pipes of the third Jimmy Saville regiment, The Seventh Finsbury Parks and finally Harry Hill himself will address the crowd with the body of the crow and give you your instructions for the year.
Parade starts Bowkettes the bakers, High Street Staplehurst. 2.00pm. Participation fee HH$14.00
4. <u>Harry's Birthday Festival</u>
To celebrate the master's birthday we ask you to take two days off work, meet up with your families, buy each other inappropriate gifts, argue, watch the guns of navarone and roast the crow with potatoes, chops and all the trimmings. Sild starter, Jelly and Ice Cream for afters.
Tickets HH$23.00
Registration fee HH$7.00

MEMENTOES AND RELICS

Sometimes it helps to concentrate on the master if you have something to remind you of him or something he has touched personally.
*Harry Hill Key Ring HH$14.00
*Stouffer the Apostle Lamp HH$12.00
*Harry Hill Aquarium HH$13.00
(no available example)
*The Master and his disciples bendy toys HH$4 each or HH$20 for the set of six. (no current samples available).

*Harry Kills the crow.
Celebrate this most important of events to us all with this bas relief of the crow killing in pure porcelain. A fine bone china plate from the Banbury Mint, hand painted with Gold Leaf edging. (Warning the glazes on this plate are highly toxic. Do not eat off the plate or death will occur. For decorative purposes only)
Plate; HH$80 Stand; HH$12.00

Barrie Gosney
Flat 4, The Albany
Piccadilly,
London WC1

Dear Bootsie,
Not the green coat, is a grey coat I lost. I've never worn a green coat in my life. You're quite sure that the footage shows me in a coat because my suit jacket is slim fitting and appears long and may be mistaken for a coat. You say the footage is in black and white but surely you can guess as to the colour of the coat/jacket. On balance do you think I am wearing the green coat or the grey coat? Have I got gloves on? Are you sure it's me in this coat Bootsie? At last I feel I am getting somewhere with this coat thing.
Yours ever

Barrie
x x

Barrie

PS Am I going in or coming out?
PPS What is the colour of the coat that has been handed in?

ALAN'S P♥EMS TO THE FEMALE TV PRESENTERS

DEAR DE DEAR LORRAINE KELLY
MY NAME IS ALAN AND I AM A BIG FAN OF YOURS
I AM UNABLE TO WORK DUE TO BOILS. HEAR IS A POEM
I HAVE WRITTEN WITH YOU IN MYNDE. PLEASE
SEND SIGNED 10 BY 8 PHOTO TO ALAN AND ALSO
SIGN ENCLOSED PAGE FROM RADIO TIMES [PLEASE
SIGN ALONG TOP NOT TO ALAN JUST SIGN IT PLEASE]
AND SIGN TO POSTCARDS [ENCLOSED]
YOURS,
ALAN XXXXXXXX

To KELLY BROOKS OFF BIG BREAKFAST

TO KELLY
I'VE OFTEN SEEN YOU ON THE TELLY
YOU LOOK ANXIOUS, A FRIGHTENED CAT
UNCOMFORTABLE IN DENISE'S HAT
JUST RELAX !
AND LET YOUR OSSIE CHARM
THE AUDIENCE TO DISARM
BUT ALSO LISTEN TO PEOPLE YOU ARE
INTERVIEWING OR WHAT'S THE POINT
KELLY ?

P.S. IS JOHNNIE BLACKMAILING YOU?
SOMETHING IN YOUR PAST?
LET ME KNOW [HARRY] & STRICTIST
CONFIDENCE — CAN PULL STRINGS

F'AO ANNE ROBINSON

OH ANNE,
I'M YOUR N° ONE FAN
I LOVE WATCHDOG TOO
YOU'RE THE "DOG" I LIKE TO WATCH

[AND I BET YOU'D BE GOOD IF YOU HAD FAULTY GOODS TO TAKE BACK
NO ONE WOULD EVEN QUESTION IT; MONEY BACK STRAIGHT AWAY
BUT DO NOT ABUSE IT ANNE]

TO LORRAINE KELLY

LORRAINE, LORRAINE,
YOU ARE THE MAIN
ONE, WHEN IT COMES TO GMTV
BUT YOU DO NOT NEED TO BE GENETICALLY MODIFIE
AS PA LARKIN SAYS
" YOU ARE PERFICK "

TO JENNY BOND (BBC) NEWSDESK

JENNY BOND, JENNY BOND, JENNY BOND
THE NAME IS BOND;
JENNY BOND
LICENSED TO READ THE NEWS
OH JENNY, JENNY
A MONNEY PENNY
THING IS GOING ON WHEN YOU READ THE NEWS AT ME
THERE? A HINT OF VAL SINGLETON THERE,
THE MAKE-UP THE GREASEPAINT AND HAIR
AND THE ROAR OF A BEAR [THAT YOU ARE REPORTING ON]
SO PRIM, JENNY BOND
YOU ARE CERTANLY A PROPER JENNY
BOND
  JENNY
    BOND

TO ANNE DIAMOND

OH ANNE!
I'M YOUR NUMBER 1 FAN
I SUPPORTED YOU THROUGH ALL THE MAYHEM
AT TV -
-A.M.
AND WAS SORRY TO HEAR ABOUT YOUR HUSBAND RUNNING OFF
[AFFAIR WITH] A YOUNGER GIRL [DISC JOCKEY ON "VIRGIN" RADIO]
HE DESERVED THAT BLACK-EYE IF YOU ASK ME

TO GABBY ROSLIN

OH GABBY!!
I LIKE TO STROKE YOUR HAIR LIKE A TABBY
AND, AS I DID SO, MAYBE YOU WOULD ARCH YOUR BACK
LIKE A TABBY CAT
YOU WISE-ASSED SASSY LADY!
P.S. BUT I DO NOT LIKE THE NEW SHOW. I THINK YOU'RE BETTER
WHEN DEALING WITH MORE WEIGHTY ISSUES LIKE DEATH AND/OR
DISEASE ETC., AS YOU SEEM TO CONNECT WITH PEOPLE.

I recently discovered this cache of love poems that big brother Alan had been writing to the female TV presenters. Although I realise now that I had been helping to write them, at the time I thought it was a school project. Still, you get few enough opportunities to meet ladies in this life and there was never a thing more likely to turn a lady's head than a simple POEM.

Reader
Please note: I helped Alan on some of the poems.
— Harry

Phil Harris
Kingsway
London

Barrie Gosney
Flat 4 The Albany
Piccadilly, London WC1

Dear Barrie,
Thank you for your letter and sorry to hear of your missing coat, I can only imagine the trouble it is causing you as I am fortunate never to have lost a coat although I remember losing my hat and that was trouble enough.
As to the weather saturday last but one as I recall it was fine with the threat of squally showers. I have dropped a line to the Meteorological office to see if they can check their records, in the meantime did you video the film on saturday last but one because often one finds it includes the tail end of the weather report before the film. This might hold the definitive answer although whether you would definitely wear your coat on the off chance of squally showers I do not know. Knowing you as I do, I suspect you would probably chance it in the jacket and take your pacamac. After all you do not want a heavy top coat in fine weather.
Anyway Barrie best of luck with the coat.
Yours

Phillip

Barrie Gosney
Flat 4 The Albany
Piccadilly, London WC1

To Jill Gosney-Peters,
"Sampfire"
Chalfont St Giles
Bucks

Dear Jill
You know that coat, the grey one you bought me at Simpsons? Well I've lost it Jill. I think I left it at the Carlton but cannot be sure even if I was wearing it that night - Saturday last but one. As my ex-wife you know me as well as anyone - am I the sort of man to go out in weather described as "Fine but with occasional squally showers" in just my jacket and pacamac or would I wear the grey coat? Phil Harris thinks I would probably make do with the pacamac but I'm not so sure. The gloves were in it as well, the brown Dents that Jaquii bought me in Haiffa. Would you give it some thought? Love to John.

Barrie
x x

Barrie

PS It was grey and not green that coat

34

After my recent brush with the Crow I have started a campaign to have the breed recognised officially as Vermin for the year 2000.

THE CROW
A MODERN DAY
INTERPRETATION

★Campaign To Have Crows Registered As Vermin 2000★

Name	Address
Ken Livingstone	14 Oakwood Manor Hampstead
Bill Tammy	14 Temple Goat Lancs
Princess Margaret	Flat 4 (Top Bell) Frap Mansions W1

There are ample reasons why the Crow should be included on the vermin list and here are a few.

1. Ugly - Crows are all one colour - black. So is the blackbird yeah, but at least the blackbird has a different coloured beak (yellow).

2. Stink - Ever got close to a crow? Don't bother but if you do the first thing that hits you is the stench - it almost knocked me over during my brush with the Crow. It's somewhere between a pile of horse sick and Jeremy Beadle's armpit - frightfest!

3. Spread SCURF™ - By landing on your head the crows trap tiny SCURF™ particles under their claws and spread it to the next scalp they land on. As we know there is as yet no proper cure for SCURF™ although cleaning up your lifestyle helps. Not only scurf, crows by their evil "take, take" life style spread constipation, headaches and gut rot.

4. Noisy - But not in a nice way like the cuckoo or the owl, they don't even bother trying to whistle, they simply open their beaks and let the ugly, lazy cry guff out "Caw! Caw! Caw!" which literally translated means "Take! Take! Take!"

5. Hop - Nor do they walk with any dignity, no they have bad posture and hop or prance like some kind of avian Mick Jagger character.

6. Steal babies - Crows have been known, on many occasions, to steal human babies from under their owner's noses as these newspaper cuttings show;

Where do they take our babies?
We all know that crows steal our young but where do they take them? It is thought that the crows take the babies and bring them up as their own - schooling them in bird like antics such as weaving, eating grubs and prancing. These crowbabies may well be amassing in our trees to form a go-between generation for the birds and humans/other mammals.

Daily Mail

Baby Stolen
From Pram By Crow

...baby was stolen by a ...ow today, from a ...am in St. Albans. ...he pram was left ...utside with the baby ...n it and the crow just ...sort of snatched it out.

TIMES

CROW-BABY-STEALER
Another baby has been stolen by a crow

from under the nose of its parents. This time, in Stafford a baby was relaxing on a blanket and was just snatched by a big black crow.

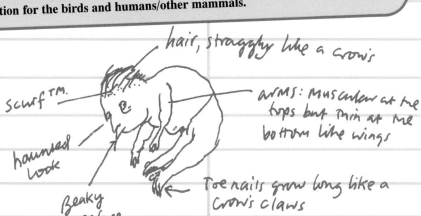

hair, straggly like a crow's

scurf ™.

haunted look

Beaky typeface like a crow's

ARMS: muscular at the tops but thin at the bottom like wings

Toe nails grow long like a crow's claws

The CrowBaby

KENN FORD POSITIONS

Michael Barrymore's Night Off

Name:	Kenn Roy Ford
Age:	73
Education:	That progressive school in Devon where the headmistress was a streaker Oxford University 1952-57

The Pigeon Fancier's Return

Jobs:		
	1958-64	Nude modelling for amateur gardening
	1965-69	Leg modelling
	1969-72	Miscellaneous streaking
	1972-78	Life model for Joy of Sex books
	1977	Streaked through Queen's Silver Jubilee Celebrations
	1977-78	In H.M. Prison for streaking offences
	1979	More Joy of Sex
	1980-83	Solid Silver Positions of the Seventies Roadshow Tour with wife Anna
	1984	Streaked through Royal Wedding of Charles and Diana
	1985	Prison again for streaking
	1986	Receives OBE from Queen for services to nude modelling and streaking
	1987	Suffers minor stroke whilst streaking
	1998	Turns down offer to front Eurotrash
	1998	Joins Harry Hill for the late night TV Sex Show "Harry Hill"
	1999	Joins Harry on Sild P.I. to help promote autobiography: "Streaking and Stroking: My Story" by Kenn Ford

The Tapir

The Insurance Scam

Funky Mat

Monkey Fat

The Ferret's Handbag

**The Lion The Witch
and the Anthony Worrall Thomson**

The Sild's Retreat

**Richard Madeley's
Revenge**

The Cardinal's Consent

The Lee & Herring

Trouble in the Balkans

The Vale of York

**The Scurf Sufferer's
Whimper**

**The
Firestarter**

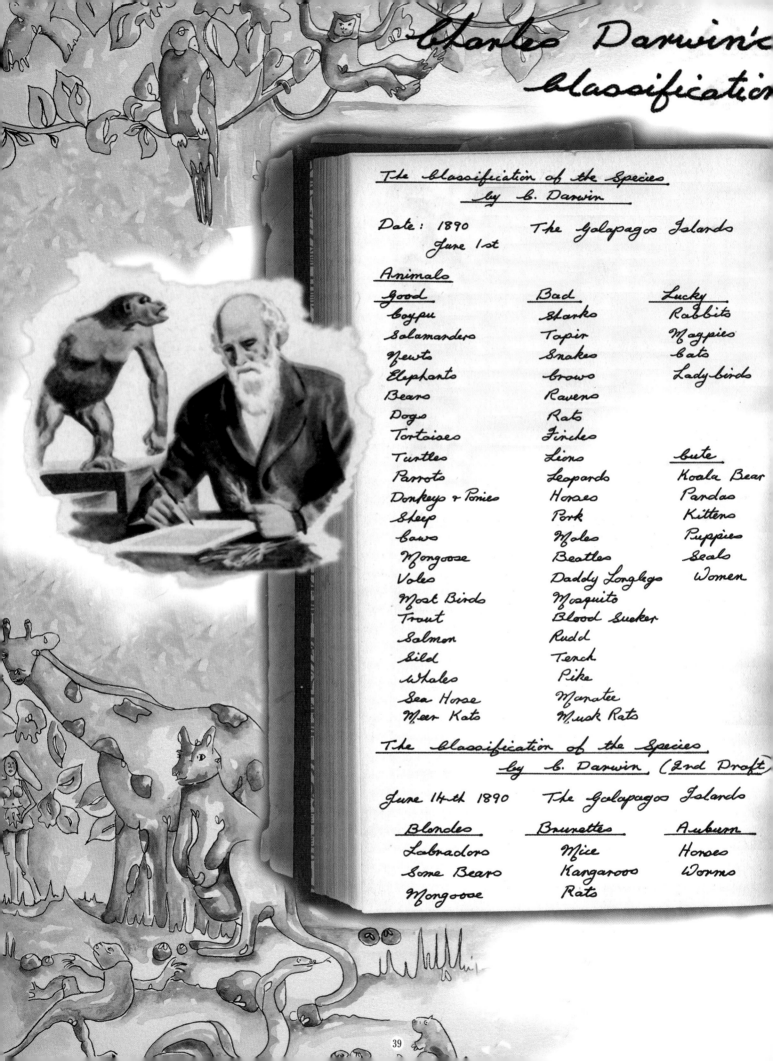

The Classification of the Species
by C. Darwin

Date: 1890   The Galapagos Islands
      June 1st

Animals

Good	Bad	Lucky
Coypu	Sharks	Rabbits
Salamanders	Tapir	Magpies
Newts	Snakes	Cats
Elephants	Crows	Lady-birds
Bears	Ravens	
Dogs	Rats	
Tortoises	Finches	
Turtles	Lions	**Cute**
Parrots	Leopards	Koala Bear
Donkeys + Ponies	Horses	Pandas
Sheep	Pork	Kittens
Cows	Moles	Puppies
Mongoose	Beatles	Seals
Voles	Daddy Longlegs	Women
Most Birds	Mosquito	
Trout	Blood Sucker	
Salmon	Rudd	
Sild	Tench	
Whales	Pike	
Sea Horse	Manatee	
Meer Kats	Musk Rats	

The Classification of the Species
by C. Darwin (2nd Draft)

June 14th 1890   The Galapagos Islands

Blondes	Brunettes	Auburn
Labradors	Mice	Horses
Some Bears	Kangaroos	Worms
Mongoose	Rats	

Blondes

Hamsters
Polar Bears
Golden Retriever
Lions
Ponies
Gerbils

Brunettes

Moat Dogs
Lizards
Trout

Black Haired

Chimpanzee
Gorilla
Some Bears
Labradors
Panther
Bats

Mixed

Tiger
Giraffe
Panda
Dalmatian
Badgers

Gingers

Red Squirrels
Tamarind
Salmon
Goldfish

The Classification of the Species
by C. Darwin (3rd Draft)

July 12th 1890

Animals that begin with 'P'

Partridge
Pig
Parrot
Pony
Panther
Preying Mantis
Panda
Polar Bear

The Others

Tiger   Cat   Rabbit
Beatles   Salmon   Voles
Ants   Trout   Moles
Finches   Snake   Hamsters
Budgies   Coypu   Bats
Elephant   Horse   Grass
Giraffe   Dogs   Hoppers
Donkey   Mongoose   Sild
Squirrel   Lion   Whales
Tapir
Coyote   Daddy Longlegs
Hyena   Ladybird
Moles   Magpie

Dear Mrs Darwin,
Having some difficulty with this classification of the species idea, I wonder if its a bit over ambitious. How about doing some sort of Good Bed and Breakfast Guide? Does it have to be classification of the species is what I'm saying? Check it out Now, like a funk soul Brother,
Yours,
Charles

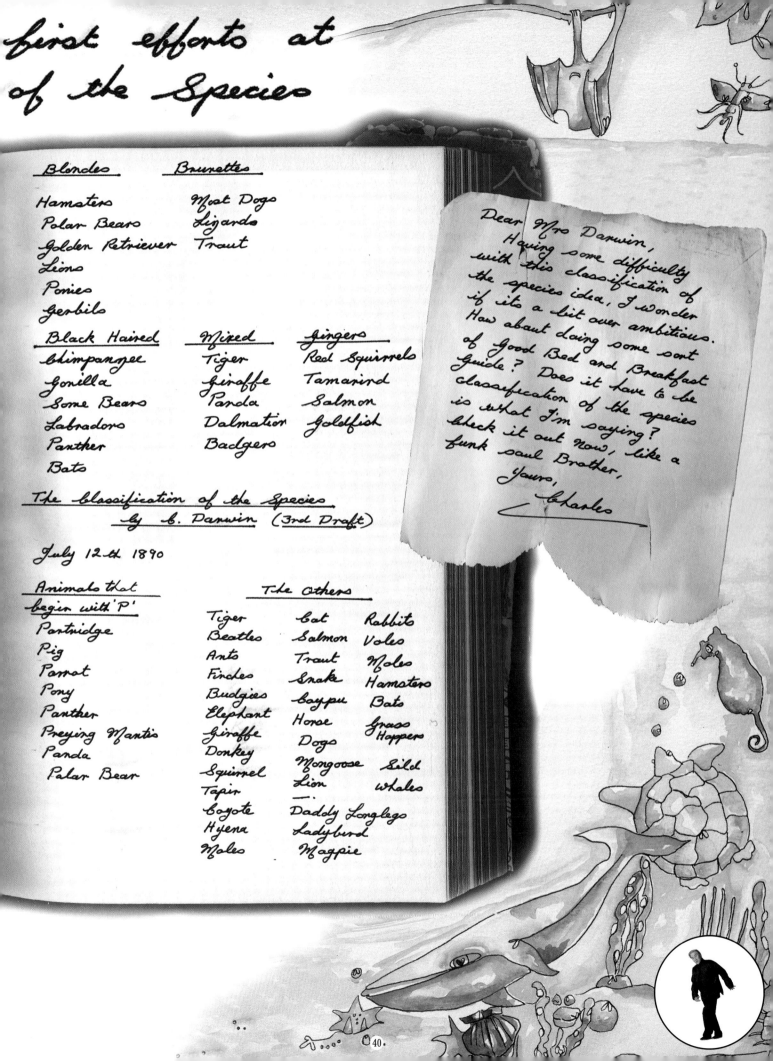

Our Wedding Day by May Sung

When we arrive in UK (freight) me so happy to meet Mr Harry. He look nothing like photo! He not got hair on head at all! His head shiny like ping pong ball! My family back in Phillipines all laugh at funny shiny head! Me did launch complaint with agency but too late! Cheque had been cashed! Mr Harry so nice, though, so strong but will not give May Sung Abbey National Book! It what marriage all about in it! To share worldly goods? Share Abbey National Book! May Sung look after book and maybe send some money to family back home for safe keeping. Mr Harry he no like to touch May Sung, he say "too soon" or "mum might see". We arrange with Vicar to bless marriage as May Sung been married before (*eight times as I found out later* - Harry) but Vicar drink lager drinks in pub and go whole way - full UK Wedding. Normally they just have quick service in Registry Office and two nights in bed and breakfast. Soon after wedding come happiest day of my life - me get full UK passport through! Ha ha!

Order of service
As Congregation file in "The Theme from Animal Hospital"

Hymn
Fight the Good Fight

The Marriage

The Prayers
Lord have mercy upon us
Christ have mercy upon us
Oh Christ what have I done
What done me have I Oh Lord
That I would enter into this with mine eyes open
Not seeing the obvious pitfalls ahead
All she's after is my money
If only Lorraine Kelly had answered my letter of proposal
She looks like she's got a few bob stashed away
I saw the interior of her house in Hello once and I could live with that stuff
Oh lord hear my prayer
Amen

Psalm 23
Yea though I walk in the valley of the shadow of death I will fear no evil
For thine is with me
Thine rod and staff to comfort me etc.

During the signing of the Registers "Where Do You Go To My Lovely" by Peter Sarstedt will be played.

At the Exit of the Bride and Groom "The Theme from Eastenders"

My Day by Harry Hill

I awoke on the morning of my nuptials rather the worse for wear. Burt and Alan had come round for the stag the night before and two bottles of Thunderbird (between us, silly) and a raunchy video film (Porkies 2, have you seen it?). Well it was quite a night and after they had gone, and I'd watched Newsnight, I turned in, surprised that I only had to "get up" once in the night.

Well the next day the hire car arrived, a lovely cream Mondeo (although I hadn't expected to read "Hertz" on the side) and made our way over to the Register Office. They were all there - Mum, Alan and Burt. Well, May Sung did look a picture, the month on antibiotics had done the trick and it's amazing the bits and pieces you can pick up in the secondhand shops - particularly if you go to a good area. May Sung had said that, in keeping with women's lib, she didn't want to say "Obey" in the service, and insisted that I say it instead.

You are invited to the wedding of
May Dung Sung and Harry Roy Hill
at Wandsworth Registry Office
and afterwards at the Bernie Inn, Lavender Hill.
6th September 1998, 12.30
Dress : Sombre
R S V P

The photographer took a few snaps for posterity - his monkey too tired to pose, and then we headed for the function room of the Bernie - we had tried in the interest of economy to keep the numbers down but inevitably if you invite one person you have to invite another and so on and the numbers somehow managed to creep up to fifteen. (I paid for the drinks and main courses but starters, puddings and coffees were extra.)

After the reception we travelled Eurostar to Dover, got off and got the ferry to Calais where we had a lovely French Lunch - she the Biftec and Frites, I the Omelette and a lovely glass of Rosé Wine (you know the type where the bottle comes in a sort of basket) and then to keep the theme going we got a couple of French style Yoghurts from the supermarket and had those while in the queue for the ferry back. We certainly made the most of the last days of duty free - 200 tabs for me (I don't smoke and can't abide the habit in others but you can always shift a few packets round the pubs). We had planned to stay in a travelodge on the way back but thought better of it - well, there's nothing quite like your own bed is there?

CHOOSE YOUR CAVY

Merlin - Fast over rough terrain, though lacks the insight to be a real champ.

Faggot - Naive cavy, lacks pace.

Taggart - Promising newcomer, shown good early form, though inexperienced.

Midnight Earmine Melody - A skittish cavy bitch prone to unpredictable soilings.

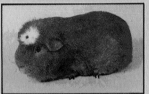

Spot - The Suzanne Dando of the cavy world : hard, tanned and rarin' to go.

These are your players
Let the game commence

Rules

1. No more than 40 players.
2. If a cavy passes one go that go automatically transfers
to the one-but-anticlockwise player.
3. The cavy with the least amount of problems wins.
4. Cavys must be clean about the house.
5. Soiling by cavys results in automatic disqualification.
6. No G.M. Cavys (G.M. – Genetically Modified).
7. Random urine tests
may be carried out on any cavy.

GOOD LUCK!

Big Bread Lunch
Accept 2 grains

Distracted
by beautiful
hamster
Miss a go

Crack open a
brazil nut
and get it out whole
Advance 2 places

Appear on
Animal
Hospital and
goosed by Rolf

Butter on Path
Advance 1 Place

Grooming Bay
Pay 2 Grains

Attacked
by a
Psychopath
Lose 3
Grains

Facing Wrong Way
Miss a go

Have Litter
of 3 Babies
Miss a go

Great tufts
of hair
fall out
Advance to
Grooming Bay

CAVY-

START

Gareth and Tasmin's Laugh In

More hilarious after dinner jokes

HOW THE NEWS IS MADE

WHAT GOES ON BEHIND THE SCENES

AT CHANNEL FOUR NEWS

daaa, Da da Daaah Dah Dahha dah Dah dah daaaah Da da da! The familiar
ins of the Channel Four News theme ring out in over a thousand television
up and down the country.

od evening, I'm Zeinab Badawi," says a smart lady with black hair - if it's
nab Badawi doing it that night (although admittedly she hasn't done it for
hile) or "Good evening, I'm Jon Snow and here is the news," says a white
ed old man standing, slightly stooped if it's Jon Snow that is doing it (and
easingly it is).

how does a thing that happens become news?
's go back to when it was that the thing happened.

Opm

two o'clock in the afternoon and David Beckham, the young football
er for Manchester United Football Club, is seen emerging from Chris's,
Barbers in Northcote Road, with a slightly different look. His moustache
been shaved off completely and his by now trademark sideboards have
n re-shaped to point in a backwards direction. On top of that his eyebrows
e become knotted in the middle and fleas dance about on his shoulders. In
rt he's a mess.

w, at the moment this thing is just something that has happened but is it
rthy of a place in the news?

1pm

aight away the phone rings in the main phone centre of Channel Four
ws headquarters. "Bring! bring! bring! bring!" It goes, "Bring! bring! bring!
ng! bring!" The phone barks out its warning cry, "Bring! bring! bring!
ng! bring! bring!" Impatiently stuttering its clarion call, "Bring! bring!
ng! bring! bring! bring!" "Hello newsroom? David Beckham, hair re-
ping incident? I'll tell the guvnor!" The young boy runs hastily down the
rridor, stopping only to be sick from fatigue. He knows a hot story has come

through and his guvnor must know about it before anyone else so that
Channel Four News can have what is known as a "Scoop". Just as ice cream
or mash potato are scooped so, it seems, is news - like so much doggie dirt from
the pavement with one of these pooper scoopers.

"Boss! Beckham...story..." the boy croaks waving a piece of paper with some
scribbles on it shortly before dying from extreme exhaustion. The head of
Channel Four News Darcy Fortinbrass (yes, the third, less well known bald
brother from Right Said Fred) reads the scribbles as the boy's body is quietly
removed for autopsy. "Hmmm David Beckham, hair re-shaping incident,
Northcote Road." His mind furrows as if ticking over like a clock or taxi
meter, even. The thoughts cascade across his brain like sands through an egg
timer or splash upon the shore of his cerebrum like the tide coming in. "Was
he hurt? Is the hair salvageable? How has Posh Spice (David Beckham's wife,
Posh Spice, who is one quarter of the pop sensation The Spice Girls who have
had a string of hits both here and in America. Hits like "Mama" and
"Wannabe" and "Put Your Mittens On And Let Your Thumb Run Free")
taken it? Is there a Royal angle?" All these and countless more must be taken
into consideration before a thing that has happened can become news.
Gradually a crowd of spaced out freaks gather outside the glass cage that is
Darcy's office. Their noses pushed hard against the glass
looking for any sign of what he might be thinking. He
twitches, takes one last swig of Brain Food Tonic, leaps
from his chair and cries, "Newsy! Newsy! Newsy!"
The freaks leap in delight and dance manically to the
sound of Joe Boxer's "Boxer Beat" which
psychologically prepares them for their ordeal. A young
mother approaches the glass and wipes away the eager
journalists' nose trails.

Time is ticking away like a clock.

It is already 3.30.

"Francesca, go to Northcote Road, see if you can get a comment from the hairdresser!"

"Yes boss!"

"Arnie? How much petrol you got in the Cortina?"

"Half a tank boss."

"Think it'll get you to Beckham's place?

"I'll try boss!"

With that Arnold Barrymore (less well known brother of Michael Barrymore the TV presenter, who in 1995 admitted drugs and alcohol abuse and also hosts Strike It Lucky) flies from the conservatory of the news room and to the slate grey Cortina estate that waits outside. Its powerful V8 engine roars into life. There is a skid of wheels on the hard black surface of the road which is known as tarmac and the vehicle disappears in the direction of Buckinghamshire.

"We'll have to move your report Peter," says head of hairdressing related stories, Channel Four News, Natty Jackson to Peter Sissons who has spent the last two days researching a piece on his own hair and how it responds to tousling. "Stuff that!" says Sissons, gobbing a large boule of spittle into Jackson's face. He wipes the secretion away with a wet wipe and stares after Sissons - he knew he would take it badly but this story was hot. "Dammit Peter! Why do you care so much about it all?" Peter Sissons glances round and shrugs. Natty leans forward and whispers to his assistant, "Could someone take Peter's shoelaces and belt and put him on 24-hour observation, I'm worried about him."

It is now 4.27 and a typically busy day for news. The stories trickle in like sand. The Trades Union Congress in session... Adam Ant launches sandwich bar... Princess Anne arrested at Bradford Airport with a nugget of heroin with a street value of 4 million pounds... Hospital staff threatening industrial action... Crow snatches a baby - the usual mixed bag.

A small knot of people gather around Moira Stewart who is receiving make up treatment for an autocue burn. She leant too close to the autocue in the early evening news and burnt the words "That report

from Nick Hyam" into her forehead. The people at Channel Four seeing whether this unholy tattoo can be masked using modern m up techniques before deciding on whether to make a hostile takeo bid on Stewart.

"I'll need three minutes on the Beckham case - we're leading with Barks Natty Jackson.

"What about the Anne drugs seizure at Bradford?" asks his num two Sharon "Brainy" Coogan.

"Lead with Beckham, and build to Anne's drugs," snaps Jack sounding a bit like the noise a dog might make.

The teleprinters were by now spluttering out details of hairdressing incident all over the building. It seems he'd asked for usual haircut but had a cold and was misinterpreted.

Peggy Ruff, vision mixer on the Channel Four News, advised t this was unlikely - "More likely deliberate bad haircutting". But story's bones were now beginning to flesh out with meat.

"Get Nicky Clarke in a cab and over to the studio NOW!" Coo neighs like a horse.

It is now 4.58 and Jon Snow is busy in matron's office having piles dressed. Piles - or Haemorrhoids, to give them their proper na - are varicose veins of the anal canal. When these veins prolapse th can become extremely painful and even thrombose, requiring hosp admission. Jon has developed them from years of sitting down read the news at us and now insists on standing to read the ne occasionally sitting on a soft, pliable ring donut of rabbit pelts to e his posterior. These dressings completed, he will be wheeled on trolley into make up where his face is decorated to look like him each strand of hair is placed manually into the scalp.

Then news comes in that Fortinbrass has stalled at the traffic lig and flooded the engine. It's unlikely now that he will be able to the interview, the shots they need and get them down to Boots back, developed in time for 7 O'clock and Natty decides to rely local eyewitness accounts and amateur video footage. Meanwh Nicky Clarke has arrived but has caught his hair in the ashtray of car and the Fire Brigade are called to cut him free. Momentarily Na considers opening with the Nicky Clarke story but dismisses it as really newsy as much as what happened to Beckham.

e control room central receives information that Beckham will hold
oorstep press conference at 8 minutes past 7. Sisson, who is openly
eping now is persuaded to fly by helicopter over David Beckham's
use and be dropped on a bungee line, during the press conference
king his questions on each bounce past Beckham's face. Two blue -
y Ford Cortina estate cars laden with camera equipment and bungee
e and strappings set off with Sissons in the back towards Richard
anson's balloon launch pad for the trip.

09

chnicians in the newsroom loop up the spools of film that is used to
y the news out on.

30

Snow has his 20 minute nap and buffet during which he is fed
ffet food through a nasogastric tube - he is old now and frail but still
the ball. His memory banks flick back like a channel changer on a
rtable TV to his past glories - and he can now almost smell the acidic
grance of the hair lacquer of Monica Lewinsky. "Oh ha ha hee John,
u are so wise." She scoffed a pie down in one. "Jon! Time to run the
ms!" He is awoken with a powerful jolt of 200 joules of DC electric
rrent to his heart as his back-up team get him going.
e roughly assembled items are read through briskly before we, the
blic, even hear them, so that the news is not news to the news
iders - they have heard it before otherwise they may appear startled
d look frightened or weep.

55

appears the Princess Anne Smack Swoop is a red herring, what the
lice found was about fifteen vanilla airwick solids that had become dried
d fused together and the story has to be dropped. The Nicky Clark
ry? Peggy Ruff advises against. "Better to not do that," she says.

58

e computer in cubicle 4 starts spewing the first shots of Beckham,
lieved to be taken outside the hairdresser's showing wisps of the
ngled mane and the wreckage of hair on the floor around him.

59

e teleprompter is wound up.
e teleprompter is a machine that is used to make it look like the
wsreader is remembering the news and consists of a roll of soft paper
und around a card cylinder with words printed on it that is carefully
wound by a girl with a handle. All the stories and footage is in place
w but there is still no sign of Peter Sissons' balloon.
tty Jackson sits in the control room confronted by a TV so he can
atch the news. He fiddles with a button, and exclaims in canine
ngue, "Frame up camera one! Teleprint! On your marks get set..."
don't think that this is a good idea..."
hut it Peggy!" belches Jackson.
issons in place!" comes the cry from the boy earlier who hadn't died
ter all.

"Roll theme tune and start up the news!" cries Natty.
"Good evening, I'm Jon Snow and here is the news."
The boy collapses once again at his master's feet and Peter Sissons
comes crashing through the ceiling of the studio with "Let's talk about
my hair!"
It's all in a day's work for the Channel Four News...

This is an extract from Harry Hill's forthcoming book
"Taking the Sissons; The truth about late night news"
(Boxtree).

The Carlton Club
Piccadilly
London W1

Dear Mr Gosney
On reviewing the security footage I am sorry to say
that the grey coat that you describe and which I had
previously seen you wearing on the said footage is in
fact not on you but on Mr Bacon. As to the colour one
could say it was a light shade but this would fit with
green or grey or indeed beige or pink Sir.
I am not at liberty to disclose the colour of the coat
handed in saturday last but one for the obvious
reason that someone might then try to claim a coat
not belonging to them suffice to say that no grey coat
has been handed in to the attendant at our end and so
I can only suggest you try another avenue of enquiry.
As regards the gloves Mr Bacon is not wearing the
gloves in the footage although I cannot say as to your
own hand coverings.
With Best Wishes

A Bootle

Mr Arthur Bootle

1 A fifteenth century torturer would often shout "Tighten the screws! Tighten the screws!" but then so would a twentieth century DIY expert. A fifteenth century torturer would also say "Stretch! Stretch!" but also an aerobics instructor. What am I saying? I dunno. DIY and Aerobics can be like torture sometimes, I suppose.

2 Zoos. We imprison animals against their will, we prod them with sticks, we throw things at them, we try to arouse them by imitating their calls, we throw buns to them. Also there's a shop.

3 Just as travel Scrabble is a smaller version of Scrabble so are suitcases smaller versions of giant suitcases that existed hundreds of years ago?

4 Lockets are a good idea - a hard outer coating that helps to treat the sore throat and an inner liquid that just soothes and repairs deep throat soreness. Also they're a bit like sweets, aren't they?

5 If you take your watch off you find yourself still looking at your wrist for the time and this goes back to a time when your watch was on there.

6 Corpses on display in museums - what about the people they once were? With lives, families, feelings. You can see their eyes and everything. Brilliant.

7 Do we pull curtains to keep the light out or the darkness in?

8 Hey Mr Beggar with your bowl - there's more to life than soup.

9 I know people say, "What's in a name?" But if I find people called "Chris" tend to be really helpful, people called Susan really sweet and people called Hitler tend to shout a lot and be bad.

10 Purses - small carriers of money? Or suitcase eggs?

11 Fish paste is not stuff for sticking two fish together, no, if you're making Siamese fish it's superglue, but make sure that both surfaces are free from dirt and grease.

12 I'd done so well with mum's shopping list but how was I to know that an eyebrow pencil was not a novelty pencil in the shape of an eyebrow.

13 All you eat is fish Mr Eskimo and you don't need a fridge, no, what you need Mr Eskimo is DENTAL FLOSS and a TIC TAC!

14 When a child is just sitting there going "Help help help" do they mean something else or is it just a cry for help?

15 Bird watching is fine but I don't think anyone really believes it reduces bird crime. We've just got to face up to the fact that some birds are just plain bad.

16 If only the man who invented the milk bottle could see all the different types of milk containers now available. Let's list them - the plastic bottle, the cardboard carton... they're the main ones.

17 The thing with the earth right, it's round right so what's the point of ironing? Come to think of it what's the point of anything, man?

"**Funny** to think that clothes happened just because **a leaf** got caught somewhere."

BRAIN THOUGHTS of BIG ALAN

"The thing about **history** is, in the olden times, people were much <u>smaller</u> and also the ground was lower down."

"If you keep **a kitten** in a drawer does it stay a kitten because of the confined space or do you just end up with **a drawer shaped cat**"

Barrie Gosney
Flat 4, The Albany
Piccadilly,
London WC1

Dear Bootle,

Re Disappearance of Grey Coat

I hardly think a member of the Carlton Club would be around town in a pink coat and I'll thank you to treat my enquiries with the gravity according an expensive coat (from Simpsons). Will you not disclose the colour of the coat handed in? Was it a green coat?

Yours sincerely

B. Gosney

Jigsaw Faces

Here are 6 "Jigsaw" photographs of well known television personalities. Each one has part of the "jigsaw" missing - How many can you recognise? (Answers on page 88).

Barrie Gosney
Flat 4, The Albany
Piccadilly,
London WC1

Dear Greg,

Re Loss of Coat

Bootsie at the Club informs me that saturday last but one you were wearing a light coloured coat which might possibly be grey. I do not remember you having a light coloured top coat. Greg, did you pick up my coat in error? As you know the gloves and other items were in the pockets and it is these as much as the coat that I would like to see returned. We all make mistakes of this nature and I'm willing to accept that this was a minor error of coat colour or style. If you picked up the coat in error could you please let me know and I will arrange to have it picked up from your rooms.

Kind regards

Barrie
x x

Barrie Gosney

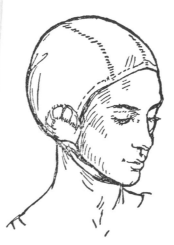

"A proper bathing cap."

Gregory Bacon
14 The Strand
London WC1

to Barrie Gosney
Flat 4 The Albany
Piccadilly, London WC1

Dear Barrie,
Thank you for your letter about the on going disappearance of your coat. You're absolutely right I do not have a grey coat or even a light coloured top coat. I can only assume that what Bootsie saw on the security footage was my pac-a-mac. As I recall saturday last but one was fine but with occasional showers in which case I would almost certainly have worn my pac-a-mac.

Yours

Gregory Bacon

Gregory

HARRY AND BURT AT HOME
THAT'S THE THIRD TIME YOU WATCHED YOUR 'THEY THINK IT'S ALL OVER' VIDEO THIS MORNING!
I KNOW BURT, BUT THE CHEMISTRY OF GOWER, HANCOCK, LINNEKAR, HIRST-
AND OF COURSE RORY McGRATH, MAKES FOR GREAT PRIME-TIME ENTERTAINMENT.
YEAH, WELL YOU CAN FORGET ANY IDEAS OF GETTING ON MAINSTREAM TV -
-YOU'RE A LATE NITE CULT COMIC- WHO FITS INTO A PARTICULAR NICHE MARKET!
I CAN! I CAN BE MAINSTREAM!
YOU CAN TELL BY THE WAY I USE MY WALK- I CAN DO MAINSTREAM, I WON'T BALK-
WE CAN DANCE-
-WE CAN SING-
WE CAN DO THE MAINSTREAM THING
WE GONNA MAKE IT
WE GONNA MAKE IT
WE WON'T BALK-
-WE WON'T BALK-
AH HAH!
HA HAH
WE CAN DO MAINSTREAM!
OH IT'S NO USE -
-I'LL NEVER BE A PRIME-TIME MAINSTREAM ACT.
OH-BY THE WAY- I NEVER MENTIONED- THERE WAS A PHONE CALL-
-THEY WANT YOU FOR 'HAVE I GOT NEWS FOR YOU'
THEY WANT ME FOR 'HAVE I GOT NEWS FOR YOU'?!
THAT'S WHAT I SAID- DIN'T I?
THIS IS IT BURT! THIS IS MY POP AT THE TOP- WHO'S THE OTHER GUEST?
"KEN LIVINGSTONE-"
THERE'S NO WAY YOU CAN LOOK GOOD ON THAT SHOW UNLESS YOU'RE ONE OF THE REGULARS-
-YOU'LL BOMB!
HMM, YOU'RE RIGHT BURT- UNLESS.... UNLESS....
YOU MEAN?
YES! BREAK INTO THE 'HAVE I GOT NEWS FOR YOU' TEAM'S FLAT AND STEAL THE QUESTIONS THE NIGHT BEFORE!
LET'S GO!
THAT NIGHT...
THIS LOOK'S LIKE IT...
14
DEAYTON HISLOP MERTON
TOMSK
E. STURTON
F. DUNAWAY
BRIAN HARVEY
BRADLEY WALSH JOE PASQUALE
YEAH! THIS THE PLACE ALRIGHT!
SHH BURT- THEY ARE SLEEPING!

Harry's Crazy Eighties Crossword

Do you remember the eighties?
Prove it! See if you can fill in the blanks.

ACROSS

2 Conservative MP for the Vale of York (4,8)

7 across & 1 down I froth at the mouth and fear water, I am....? (6,7)

10 A big round river that doesn't go anywhere (4)

12 across & 25 down Group of fish swimming together (7,4)

14 Jimmy Nail sang "It Was A Big...." (3,2,3,3)

16 across & 26 down Bearded President of Cuba (5,5)

19 across & 22 down The smell of the greasepaint, the roar of the... (11,8)

23 Popular in the eighties, had a big hit with "Gold" - Spandau? (6)

24 Like a knife through....? (1,5)

27 You've hit...............on the head when you are right (3,6)

28 I am flat and without me there would be no such thing as a refreshing towelette. What am I? (1,6)

30 I like to press wild (5)

32 One was fat, one was thin, one called Eddie, the other Sid (6,9,4)

33 Comedy loons Vic Reeves and Bob............? (9)

DOWN

1 See 7 across

2 See 21 down

3 Which came first, me or the chicken? (2)

4 down & 31 down Brucie's greeting, "Nice to see you, to see you...." (2,3,3)

5 Pictured musician - The entertainer (5,6)

6 Tousle haired star of Jonathan Creek (8,5) (see picture)

8 Check him out now like a funk soul brother Fat Boy.... (8,6,2)

9 See 18 down

11 My first is in water, but not in river (5)

13 His name was Phil Oakey, he had one side of his hair long, the other short and was a member of the Human...... (4)

15 Dobson, once Brian May's lover, ran a pub with Dirty Den (5)

17 William Hague's wife (5)

18 down & 9 down Hawaii Five....? (7,5,4,13)

20 Glove with only thumb free, begins with M.... (6)

21 & 2 down How tickled I am Kenn and his little tiny friends (5,4,3,3,7)

22 See 19 across

25 See 12 across

26 See 16 across

29 The .... of the Town - something to do with speech (4)

31 See 4 down

Answers page 88

⑤⑦

THINGS TO DO ON A RAINY DAY

1. Get a tattoo done
2. Or an existing one removed
3. Visit an OAP and ask to borrow money
4. Phone up your local pest control officer and demand that crows be considered vermin
5. Get a petition up to give weight to the above. Start with people in your family
6. Send out some post-dated cheques
7. Tidy up the things on top of the tall boy
8. Consider a trip to the farm museum then all the reasons why not to go. Draw up a pie chart or graph
9. Start making detailed descriptions of the crows that visit your garden for when the new vermin legislation comes in
10. Look through mum's catalogues for something for her birthday
11. Cut pictures out of catalogues and make a collage of your ideal home - bread maker/foot spa/his and hers towels
12. Make a home made camcorder documentary about your room with a view to sending it in to Video Nation
13. Fake up an accident that you can film on your camcorder to send in to You've Been Framed
14. Start mixing up crow poison in anticipation of the ban

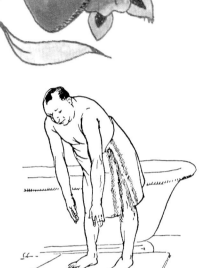

" To exercise the abdominal muscles by formal bathroom tricks."

THE NAMES THEY WISH THEY WAS BORN WITH

What's in a name?
Find out how these top names would have been better suited to their profession with a simple name change

Chefs

Ainsley Haricot-Bean
Marco Pierre White-Bait
Anthony Waffle Thompson
Gary Roast
Jamie Bath Oliver *(the sassy young chef from BBC2)*
Delia Sweet-Trolly

Some of My Favourite Shops by Noel Gallagher

Versace, Bond Street
Gucci
Asda
F. Khaminake Coca Cola Newsagents

Barrie Gosney
Flat 4, The Albany
Piccadilly,
London WC1

to Gregory Bacon
14 The Strand
London WC1

Dear Gregory,

Re Mistaken Coat
I hardly think that Bootsie would mistake a pac-a-mac for a grey Simpsons Top Coat.
Kindly return my coat.

Sincerely

Gosney

cc Arthur Bootle

" A dog will salivate at the sight of food."

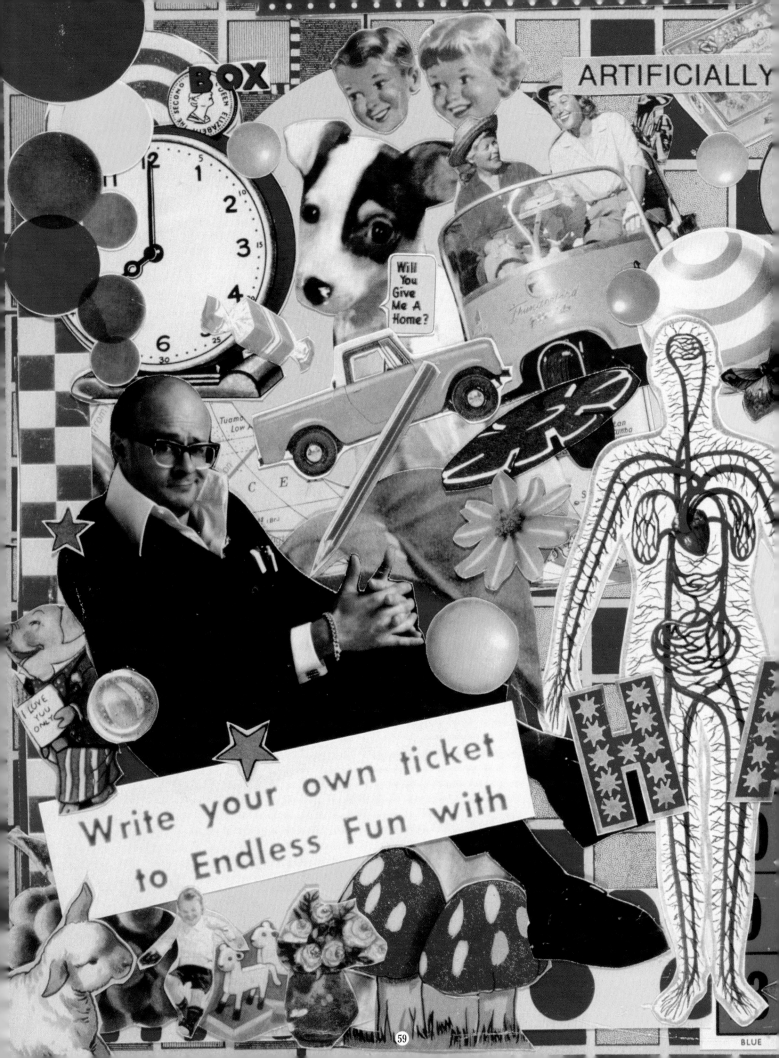

THE RIDDLE OF THE BRASS 10 INCH 2 PIN CASEMENT STAY

Harry has buried a brass 10 inch 2 pin casement stay in a secret location. If you can work out where it is from the poem and illustration this valuable prize is yours!

Whither where the brass casement stay?

Will it be Wilmslow

Whither where the brass casement stay?

Is it in Hounslow? Will it be Wilmslow?

Under earth's black heap the crow hops

Wolverhampton? Tilbury or Telford's shadow

Shrubs grow about and power stations graze

Cricket's post code in pea soup capital

But no university sits, the crow's nest falls
and its young dies

On Glasgow's pantry a popcorn effigy sits

Is it Rory? Or Burt's window?

The casement stay fits.

Under earth's black Heap

is it in Hounslow

Happy Hunting!

is it Rory?

Shrubs Grow

Brass Casement

Spot the biscuit references:
Difficult level - The three penguins stood their ground, they were asked to leave but stood united. The annual ball at sea world was a wonderful affair. Top of the bill was flipper and the three penguins enjoyed just hob-nobbing with minor celebrity seafarers.
Moderate level - What a nice evening said the three penguins just drinking Bourbon like Garibaldi. This tea's a bit rich said one of the penguins. Yes it is a rich tea.
Easy level - Would you like a Bourbon or a rich tea or a ginger nut or a jammy dodger or a digestive? said one of the three penguins.

What I like about the collection of shops at Gatwick airport is they've got a lovely villagey feel.

Never wear wooden trousers to a lumberjack conference.

It's no good catching mice in humane traps, you've got to kill one, stick its head on a cocktail stick and parade it through the mouse kingdom. Send a clear message to the other mice, 'Don't touch my cheese!'

Notice how at garden centres they put the Alpine plants on a slightly higher shelf.

Gregory Bacon
14 The Strand
London WC1

to Barrie Gosney
Flat 4, The Albany
Piccadilly, London WC1

Dear Barrie

Honestly all this fuss about a silly coat. For the last time I do not have your blessed coat. Now can we call a halt to this nonsense.

Sincerely

Gregory Bacon

Gregory

They say you can tell a lot about someone from their favourite nut;
zelnut - small, friendly to others
Almond - oval, keen to join in
Brazil - reserved, tough outer hell, difficult to get out whole.

My TV
riel is using my
V as an ariel.

Yet More BRAIN THOUGHTS

You look at the old lady with the wrinkled face, thinning hair, false teeth, then you look at a photo of the young woman, clear eyed, graceful, an inner glow and you say "Yup I'll go with the young one please."

Hilarious Dog Stories
by L. M. Hand
No.2 Douglas Learns A Lesson

Douglas was a year-old *Westie* at the training class. The problem was this, Doug kept picking fights with all the bigger "Boy" dogs. Fine with my own bitch Annie but a downright nuisance to a lot of the dogs in the class all there to learn.
Well, one evening he tried it once too often. "Woof Woof!" He had a go at Carl - the *Brindle mix*, "Woof Woof!" Now it was Mutley's turn. Well, Pat our course leader had had enough. She raced up to the little white Terrier, got him by the scruff of the neck, completely off the ground now, and yelled straight in his face, "What are you doing?!!!" She was fuming! Well, Doug didn't know where to look! The poor *West Highland White* hung his head in shame. Well, Pat put him on the ground and you could tell from his body language he'd learnt his lesson.

Break dancing is good but I think that bit where you go on your back is a bit of pure showing off.

Alan Hill
Reply Letters
from the
FEMALE TV PRESENTERS

Dear Alan,

Away widj yer ya och nos sasfenacs! Fie!
And see you neh thrimble and nacht to
see brimmy!

love Lorraine

Lorraine Kelly

03.09.99
Anne Diamond

Dear Alan,

Thank-you for your excellent poem.
How do you do that? Make the words
rhyme and that? Fantastic skills.
Excellent.
Yes, it was nice to see Mike with a
shiner I must admit.

Best Wishes,

ANNE

Kelly Brook
The Big Breakfast
London

Dear Alan,

Many thanks for your poem.
Yes, it has been a busy year for me and
I thank-you for your support.

luv kelly

K. Brook

Anne Robinson
BBC1 Television
London

Dear Alan,

Re poem.
The poem is rubbish.
Please don't bother to send any more

Sincerely

A. Robinson

A. Robinson

A. Robinson

luv kelly

The Carlton Club
Picadilly
London W1

Dear Member,

Thank you for your letter. I commisserate with you for the loss of the
coat. Unfortunately we cannot send out security footage of members to
other members. Good luck with the hunt for your pink coat.
Yours sincerely

Sir Arthur Pimm
President

y Roslin
ccadilly
ndon

ear Alan,

ow! Thanks! Really nice of you and everything
- to send the poem and I know what you mean
about the new show - but it's sort of like Jim
Will Fix It isn't it? The thing is I do just
love people, they're so interesting aren't
they?
Well Alan, Good luck in everything you do,
There's no rehearsals Right?

Ah, Bless.

Gabby x x

Gaby Roslin

Jenni Bond
BBC1
London

Dear Alan,
Many thanks for your poem.
How nice of you to think of me!
I wonder whether you would be interested
in going for a drink some time?
To discuss the poem and your work?
I finish about 9.30pm after the news.
If you're interested call me.
Work : 0171 946 0003
Home : 0181 946 0001
Mobile : 07700 900 0009
or you can reach me at my mum's on : 01632 960 0006
or her mobile is 07700 900 0003
or phone the BBC switchboard on 0171 946 0009
or my pager No 0909 879 0981
or drop me a line here or at home
Call me Alan

Love

Jenni x x x x

Barrie Gosney
Flat 4, The Albany
Piccadilly,
London WC1

to Gregory Bacon
14 The Strand
London WC1

Dear Bacon,

Re Theft of Coat

Fuss about a silly coat indeed! Jill
bought me that coat from Simpsons! I ask
you again was it your pac-a-mac Greg or
were you wearing my grey top coat? It's
easy to poke fun at somebody without a
coat when one is wearing a coat but how
would you like to be without a coat (and
gloves for that matter - along with
various unknown valuables that were in
the coat pockets) in wet or cold weather.
I have a good mind to take your coat!

Yours Sincerely

Barrie

Barrie Gosney

METEOROLOGICAL OFFICE
Tottenham Court Rd, London W1

to
P. Harris
London WC1

Dear Mr Harris,
Thank you for your enquiry. When you state
"The saturday last but one" do you mean
the third or the tenth?
Please pass on our best wishes to Mr
Grasney and hope that his coat has been
found.
Yours

Turbot
blic Relations

CELEBRITY SH

What the stars buy when they're out shopping

MONDAY
BANKHOLIDAY
TOILET ROLLS
NESPAPERS
MAX FACTOR
1 MILK
PTO

VENOS TICKLE

BARBARA WINDSOR

Shredded wheat.
Raisins.
Lettuce.
almond.
Bread Crumbs.
Springs Onions.

QUEEN MOTHER

Chicken
MINCE.
LAMB.
— " —
CAULIFLOWER
LEMONS.
ONIONS
FRUIT.
— " —

Sardines
Beet root
2 apple
Vanilla ice cream
4 oz Cotage cheese
5 Saltene Bisc .
2 Hot Dogs
Broccolly
1 panana
8.

DONATELLA VERSACE

pissa
Cocktauts
Lemonade
Green Jelly

VANESSA MAE

MEG MATTHEWS

Sausages
Cinamon
Bread
Biscules
Cakes
ham
Quish

PETER STRINGFELLOW

Phil Harris
Flat 4a Kingsway Mansions
Kingsway, London

Barrie Gosney
Flat 4 The Albany
Piccadilly, London WC1

Dear Barrie,

Am I right in thinking that you've lost a coat?
Have you tried Bootsie at the club? Could you
have left it there by mistake? If you do, could
you see whether my hat has been handed in - I
lost it three months ago and still no sign.
Kind regards

Phillip

Phillip

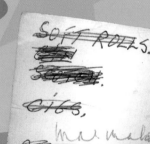

SOFT ROLLS.
marmalade
sausage
Bread
cheese
carrots
Onions
eggs

JOAN COLLINS

BOB GELDOF

```
SUGAR      66.
Greens     50
Milk       24
Cream      50
           1-9 3
```

DES O'CONNOR

```
floss
Toner.
           £20
```

BILL WYMAN

```
MILK
CLEANING
BANK  CONNECT
FRUIT    CARD
ULAY  CREAM
DENTU  HOLD
WINE!
```

GHANDI

```
koriander
fruit
veg
pep. ghee
ginger
garlic
lemongrass
muesli

angel hair spagh. (fresh)
Coke (3)
juice (orange, grapefrt)
grapefruit was (half vol).
bread
crackers
yoghurt
tofu (1)
beer
Vis
"green"   lic papier
```

DALE WINTON

```
Chick breast.
Bacon.
onion
Puree
Juice
B/Beans.
Green Brocilli.
New pots
Mince.
Vodka
Wine.

Soup.
Bread 01S.
```

DEMIS ROUSSOS

```
4 Batteries
PUREE
   YOGHORTS    BREAD
Broccoli Potatoes
   HOUMOUS     TEA
   BUNS (Currant)
      HAM BACON
        HOUMOUS
   LAMB (stewing)
SHAMPOO
BATTERIES
   CHIPOLATAS

BIRTHDAY CARDS
STEPHANIE/NASREEN
```

JOOLS HOLLAND

```
                 Tues     firelighters
                 Mussels?  Hand Lotion
P.O + Stamps.   Loaf    Beans Sponge
              Yogurt orfromf   Garlic
Carrots - Onions Potatoes  Fruit.
Salmon Mackerel Sardines.
OxO + Soup
Dover - Toothpaste
Sprouts  Thurs
veg Mince or fish
Coffee + Mate.
Lite?
Tin fruit.
Raid.
                      Tues
                   Radio
              Womans W.
                 Bella.
```

ANTON MOSSIMAN

```
FRUIT
MILK
CIGS
CHEESE.
FLORA
```

66

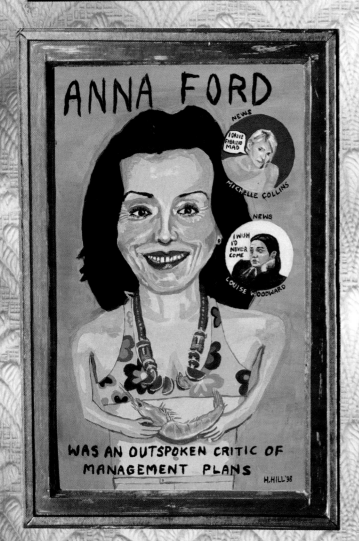

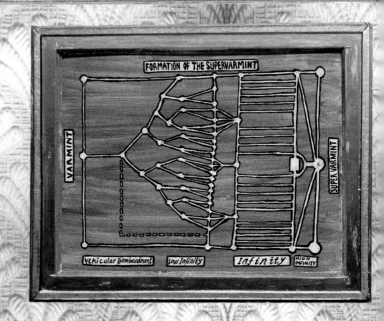

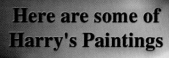

Phil Harris
Flat 4a, Kingsway Mansions
Kingsway, London

Barrie Gosney
Flat 4 The Albany
Piccadilly, London WC1

Dear Barrie,

Please ignore my previous letter. I came upon your note requesting weather information regarding the saturday last but one. On reviewing my video cassettes of that weekend I had inadvertently caught the tail end of the weather report prior to the saturday film ("Sleepless in Seattle" - the tale of love at long distance - Hanks on sparkling form but Ryan turning her usual sub-Goldie performance). Often the recorder kicks in a little early and this may be due to a slight difference in the advertised times due to live televised sporting events or merely a slight error in the time show on the recorder itself. At any rate the weather prediction for saturday last but one was "fine with scattered showers". Whether or not you would have worn your top coat based on this prediction (and I stress this was merely a prediction) remains to be seen. I hope this is helpful.

Yours Phillip

[signature]

PS Any news on my hat?

NEW NAMES FOR FILMS

Here are some new names for remakes of some classic movies

* The Island of Dr Moreau becomes *Moreau Island*
* Citizen Cane - *Cane World*
* The 39 Steps - *Steps*
* Mary Poppins - *Crazy Mary*
* It's a Wonderful Life - *It's a Wonderful Life and Then You Die*
* Dr No - *No MD*
* The Railway Children - *The Track Kids*

Hilarious Dog Stories
by L. M. Hand
No.3 Sweep - The Wayward Welshie

One sunny morning my neighbour Angela and her *Welsh Terrier* Sweep were taking a lovely stroll through local parkland. All seemed to be going very well until Sweep threw a wobbly and ran off. Well, Ange was beside herself! She searched all over the park but with no luck. Tearfully she set off for home. On arrival at her mansion block, who should she find on the doorstep, looking her right in the eye with a defiant "Chase me" gleam? Yes, you guessed it - Sweep! Talk about a scolding!

Phil Harris
Flat 4a, Kingsway Mansions
Kingsway, London

Barrie Gosney
Flat 4 The Albany
Piccadilly, London WC1

Dear Barrie,

It was the saturday last but two I was referring to.

Yours,

[signature]

Phillip

PS Are you sure that Greg has taken the hat? What proof do you offer?

Barrie Gosney
Flat 4, The Albany
Piccadilly,
London WC1

to Phil Harris
Flat4, Kingsway Mansions
Kingsway, London

Dear Phillip,

Thank you for your letter regarding the loss of my grey coat and your black trilby. You state the weather saturday last but one was predicted as being fine with scattered showers but the saturday in question is now saturday last but two. Which saturday are you referring to? To be honest Phil the whole business is academic as it seems that Greg Bacon has stolen my coat and I shouldn't wonder your black trilby.

Your fellow victim

[signature]
xx

Barrie

"*The more absurd types of collars.*"

ADULT PANTO TITLES

Thinking of producing an adult style panto
like Jim Davidson's Sinderella?
Here are some possible titles

1 Boobs In The Wood (Babes In The Wood)
2 Aladsin (Aladdin)
3 Ali Booba and the 40DD (Ali Baba and the Forty Thieves)
4 Dick Whittinsin (Dick Whittington)
5 Puss-sin-Boobs (Puss In Boots)
6 Mother Boobs (Mother Goose)
7 Jack and the Boob sin Stalk (Jack and the Beanstalk)

SIT-COM TITLES

Writing a sit-com along the lines
of Babes in the Wood about three girls
sharing a flat in St. Johns Wood?
Here are some possible titles -

1 Birds in the Bush (Shepherds Bush)
2 Tott's Forest (Epping)
3 Common Girls (Clapham)
4 Darling Buds of Grays Inn Road
   (Self explanatory)
5 Beauties and the East (Eastend)
6 Cows at Graze (Grays Inn Road again)

Gregory Bacon
14 The Strand
London WC1

to
Barrie Gosney
Flat 4 The Albany
Piccadilly
London WC1

Gosney,
For the last time I never touched your stupid
coat, retract your accusation or I will take the
matter further.

Barrie
x x

Bacon

SOME GM FOODS
I'D LIKE TO SEE THE
SCIENTISTS MAKE

1 Mushy Peas -
No need to mush them
now, but how do we pick 'em?
Just suck them off the trees
with a hose - tasty, but messy!

2 Potato that's cooked already -
It just grows on the plant cooked.
Careful when picking though - them's hot

3 Radioactive Pears - So annoying when you can't
find a nice juicy conference pear at night.
These glow in the dark

4 Poisonous Pears - Euthanasia's coming back
in a big way, so here's a pretty way of doing it.
Make your last memory a juicy pear then bam!
Out cold, just like that.

5 Eggs With Legs - You got to catch 'em to eat 'em.
Lose weight as you eat eggs.

6 Suicidal Sheep - They sense
when they're ready for slaughter
and you wake up to find them
hanged in their shed.
No mess, no note, no worries.
Apart from brief anxiety of "Could
we have done more for them?"

**General note
for the boffins:
Just make
everything bigger,
cheaper and last
longer please.**

My Hobby *by Meg Matthews*

For years now I have been collecting and making peg dolls and although me and Noel's hous "Supernova Heights" in London's fashionable St John's Wood has been decked out by one Britain's top interior designers with jacuzzi bath, the latest pop art posters and music studi for Noel, I have one room, my "peg room", which I have set up in olde worlde style (spinnir wheel in the corner etc.) so that I can just sit and make my peg dolls.

Sometimes I prefer to spend an evening "pegging" as I call it, than go to a fancy awards ceremony or fashion parade! It's got to the stage where Noel jokingly calls me "Pegg" Matthews.

Here are some of my favourite peg dolls:

My Hobby *by Prince Naseem*

Ever since I was a boy growing up in Swindon I have made Easter cards for my mum. It seem to me that a home made card says a whole lot more than a shop bought - however much yo spend. Although I bought my mum her own house and Mercedes car last year, it is the Easter cards that she eagerly anticipates.

Here are some of mum's favourites:

My Hobby *by Keith Flint of The Prodigy*

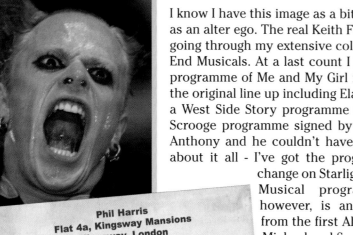

I know I have this image as a bit of a wild one, a tearaway if you will, but I see this very muc as an alter ego. The real Keith Flint, at home, likes nothing better than going through my extensive collection of programmes from the West End Musicals. At a last count I had forty-five ranging from an early programme of Me and My Girl in the forties, right up to Cats with the original line up including Elaine Page. Other highlights include a West Side Story programme signed by Kiri Te Kanawa and a Scrooge programme signed by Anthony Newley himself. I met Anthony and he couldn't have been nicer! I'm pretty dogged about it all - I've got the programme for every single cast change on Starlight Express! The one West End Musical programme that still eludes, however, is an original cast programme from the first Albery run of Phantom - with Michael and Sarah Brightman. Can anyone help?

Phil Harris
Flat 4a, Kingsway Mansions
Kingsway, London

Greg Bacon
14 The Strand
London WC1

Dear Greg
Kindly return my trilby
Yours sincerely,

Phillip

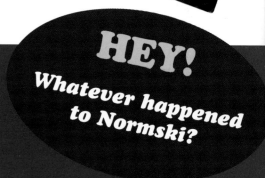

HEY!
Whatever happened to Normski?

"A CUT-OUT AND KEEP SAVE 'EM OR SWAP 'EM"

harry hill

1 — What are the chances of that happening?

alan hill

2 — If it's too hard I can't understand it

stouffer

3 — Sorted, Respect due

burt kwouk

4 — Hey Harry this show stinks

tasmin archer badger

5 — Parade's off!

dana

6 — Turn the light off first

finsbury park

7 — Do they mean me? They surely do!

nana hill

8 — You're joking ain'tcha?

denise van outen owl

9 — Oooooooh!

barrie gosney

10 — But now please welcome Harry Hill

Nos 1-10

in a series of

17 classic

trump cards

72

"A CUT-OUT AND KEEP SAVE 'EM OR SWAP 'EM"

Name:	Burt Kwouk
Age:	4
Job:	Chicken Catcher to Harry Hill
Says:	Hey Harry this show stinks!
Top Speed:	14mph
Hobbies:	The Guns of Navarone
Weaknesses:	Parakeets, Cockatiels and other small birds

Name:	Stouffer
Age:	14
Job:	Actor
Says:	Sorted, respect due
Top Speed:	28mph
Hobbies:	Collecting banana stickers
Weaknesses:	Dana International Cat

Name:	Alan Hill
Age:	60
Job:	Unemployed due to boils
Says:	If it's too hard I can't understand it
Top Speed:	12mph
Hobbies:	Collects foil wrappers from chocolate bars
Weaknesses:	Soft patch on top of head never hardened from babyhood

Name:	Harry Hill
Age:	54
Job:	Entertainer
Says:	What are the chances of that happening?
Top Speed:	15mph
Hobbies:	Popcorn sculpture
Weaknesses:	Sild

Name:	Nana Hill
Age:	86
Job:	Taxidermist (retired)
Says:	You're joking ain'tcha?
Top Speed:	6mph (seated)
Hobbies:	Sucking the pips out of nectarines
Weaknesses:	Nil

Name:	Finsbury Park
Age:	42
Job:	Chief Scientist
Says:	Do they mean me? They surely do!
Top Speed:	30mph
Hobbies:	Romance
Weaknesses:	Chops (Pork and Lamb)

Name:	Dana
Age:	7
Job:	Catovision song contest winner
Says:	Turn the lights off first!
Top Speed:	8mph
Hobbies:	Clothes shopping
Weaknesses:	Sailors

Name:	Tasmin Archer Badger
Age:	28
Job:	Shop steward
Says:	Parade's off!
Top Speed:	22mph
Hobbies:	Basking
Weaknesses:	Expensive Jewellery

Nos 1-10 in a series of 17 classic trump cards

Name:	Barrie Gosney
Age:	65
Job:	Actor
Says:	But now please welcome Harry Hill
Top Speed:	8mph
Hobbies:	My Club
Weaknesses:	Germans

Name:	Denise Van Outen Owl
Age:	27
Job:	Presenter Owl
Says:	Ooooooooh!
Top Speed:	32mph
Hobbies:	Fast cars, P-Funk
Weaknesses:	Jay Kay Owl

It bain't half be a daft world!
Says Jonty, Harry's Country Cousin!

Hey! If rain water done come outta they sky how come it bain't got wetter on the fields! Who's supping all dat water?

Hey! When I blows me candle out at night whence I blow the fire to? I bain't be a started a blaze at yon barn were it? Suck back in a fire as soon as blow it!!!

Darn millennium bug! Like a bind weed on fourth field only on Microsoft Word! Anythin to do to stop it? Take a raisin in a pouch an dip a' water - keeps baby quiet so why not millennium bug?

Oh mudda! Blue bloomin mudda! Stealth bomber over former Yugoslavia! Jonty bain't seen nought like as such since Herbert took stick to wasps nest in yon fourth field! Jar O'Water an' a dollop o' jam sees ole waspy off. What about yon stealthy??!!

I bain't been doin' nought afore yon playstation Mario do change a supermario just for jumpin' on a mushroom? Then he kick blessed turtles? No need a mushies to kick turtles, Mario, Jonty kick cow in yon fourth when outta line and bairn be on a empty stomach!!!!!

CARE OF THE HAIR

" A thick strong growth of hair is commoner among old people in the country than in towns."

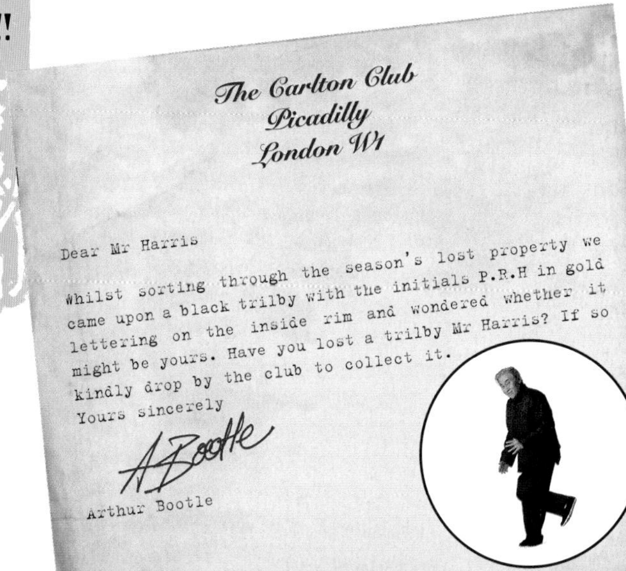

The Carlton Club
Picadilly
London W1

Dear Mr Harris

Whilst sorting through the season's lost property we came upon a black trilby with the initials P.R.H in gold lettering on the inside rim and wondered whether it might be yours. Have you lost a trilby Mr Harris? If so kindly drop by the club to collect it.

Yours sincerely

A Bootle

Arthur Bootle

The History Of The BEE GEES

Robin | Barry | Maurice

1. The Bee Gees grow up in poverty just outside Manchester. Robin Bee Gee, and Barry Bee Gee and Maurice Bee Gee. Barry and Maurice of course the identical twins in the family, although this was in the days when the criteria for qualifying as identical twins was not as stringent as it is now.

2. As they grew Robin and Maur experimented wi being women for while but found th the clothes we too loose fitti and preferred t support offered men's outfits.

3. Of course there were two other, less well known Bee Gees - Steve Bee Gee and Andy Bee Gee. Steve, seen here on the right with his early prototype for the tripod (he was later to simplify it) and Andy on the left. Andy, although keen, was unable to join the group after he hit his thumb with a hammer and they could no longer get it in the van.

4. Their father, Mr Bee Gee Senior was a very clever man - able to play the violin without looking and a man who, through the help of his hairdresser, inadvertently invented the headphones.

5. Their mother, Mrs Peggy Bee Gee, was quite happy just to sit back and let things happen. (Note the Cuban heels - popular at the time)

6. Well Robin was a terrible school truant, and would often require assistance to get him to school and in fact it would sometimes take up to four ice cream men just to get him out the door (please note the wafers and acute leg shortage that raged throughout the first part of the sixties when legs were rationed and used on a rotation system).

7. They had to walk everywhere until their father acquired a motorbike. (Note their mother was very good at ironing the fronts of the outfits but had a bit of a blind spot when it came to the backs).

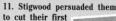

8. The Bee Gees were influenced by a little known combo The Wintons, consisting of Dale Winton a his brother. Dale, on the left, who always insisted on a spon finger before he went on. And his brother who would often ha to make do with a gerkhin.

9. The Bee Gees, formed a skiffle group here shown in their first line-up. An equal opportunities employer - as you can see they employed people of all different heights. And they all stacked away neatly one inside the other at the end of the evening.

10. It was at this time that they encountered a man who was to change the course of their lives and careers, their manager and svengali Robert Stigwood. (Note the powerful haunches, the pointed front feet, the strong sense of smell - everything you want in a manager).

11. Stigwood persuaded them to cut their first disc. Of course technology wasn't what it is today, and using two horses, primitive sixties man would simply drag a stylus up a furrow as the music belched from its underside.

12. Meanwhile back in Manchester their father had got a job in a watch.

13. But Stigwood persuaded the Bee Gees that they should seek their fortunes in Australia and they set about their journey.

14. Stigwood advis them that they wou require a change image if they we to make it dov under which the readily agreed to.

Robin | Barry | Maurice

Their support act on the first leg of at Australian tour was a little known group called e Village People who were working on a new number which they re later to change around and have a big hit with, but at this time as known as The K...M...P apostrophe.

16. Sadly at this point in the tour they received news from England that Andy Bee Gee's thumb had been taken into hospital and they had to turn the ventilator off. He lost the thumb and it took him three weeks to hitchhike home.

17. Their mother wasn't too bothered about it. She is pictured here attending a fancy dress party... dressed as a tiger.

8. Meanwhile in Manchester, their father was arrested for ying to fiddle one of those slot machines, you know the type with layers of coins and they slide in and out and the coins drop down. And it was after this particular incident that they started to put glass tops on them - and a part of our innocence died that hard October morning.

19. Andy's knees went.

20. Barry was involved in an incident with a telescope.

1. Maurice accidentally bricked himself in his own extension.

22. Robert Stigwood ballooned in weight and was hit in the head with a bread roll - or was it a croissant? We won't know until we get the ballistics back.

23. The Gulf War

24. My nan with my sister during the seventies.

25. That holiday in Pevensy Bay.

Have you got the six?

26. Me in The Pot Luck Cafe. (Burger in bun £1.06)

27. Me with my friends the penguins.

28. But they'll always remain as we remember them: The Bee Gees.

The History Of the BEEG

Harry Hill's The History Of The Bee Gees Lecture Tour. See Press For Details.

Harry's Manager IVAN PRETCHIKOV Writes

Who looks after Harry's Money?

Harry's Expenses
These are the expenses Harry incurs before he even gets the money, such as hotel bills, cars and smart clothes for me because I have a certain image to keep up. Sometimes it is necessary to throw a party for Harry but not always invite him because it would spoil it.
This is where Harry's money comes in handy.

Income
1. Radio Slots
2. TV Shows
3. Tours
4. Personality Engagements (Graham Nortons etc.)

The Carbon Dioxide of Publicity
Slush fund needed to pay off journalists who write bad things about Harry and to keep them sweet.

Harry's Tax
I pay off Harry's tax for him at the same time as mine all lumped in together.

Stouffer's Money
Stouffer is in demand and is owned exclusively by Pretchikov Entertainments and requires an ever increasing fee to ensure his participation in Harry's ventures.

My (Ivan Pretchikov)'s fee
Harry can't handle money in large chunks - it confuses him so I take it and break it down into smaller pieces and drip it through in a way he can understand.
Also I need to take 55% to cover my overheads such as paper, pens, water and oxygen - I'm not a plant, I can't just make oxygen.

Harry's bit of money that he keeps

The Oxygen of Publicity
Money required to keep Harry in the public eye so people don't forget him.
We have a whole forest that we kill every year to make leaflets and posters so people remember not necessarily his name but 'that bloke with the big collars'.

Sweets

Sild

M & S Vouchers

Chops

TRICK RIDING

Barrie Gosney
Flat 4, The Albany
Piccadilly,
London WC1

to Sir Arthur Pimm
The Carlton Club
Piccadilly

Dear Pimm,

It may have come to your notice that some time ago I lost my grey coat - and the various items in its pockets of which only the "Dents" gloves I can be entirely certain in my various attempts to track it down (including CCTV footage from your own premises) I have come to no other conclusion than Gregory Dacon stole it from the Club Cloakroom under your very nose! Can we honestly allow such immoral behaviour or like me do you feel strongly that Bacon should be struck from the Club Records and expelled upon his rear into Piccadilly?
Yours Sincerely

Barrie

Barrie Gosney

PS It would seem he also has Phil Harris' trilby
cc G Bacon, P Harris & A Bootle

Hilarious Dog Stories
by L. M. Hand

No.4 Feargal Sharky

Feargal was a five-year-old wire-haired Fox Terrier who frequented the local rec. Trouble was he fought any dog that took his fancy. A couple of times he flew at my own "wire" - Annie. Yes, strange isn't it? Turning on one of your own? That dog had problems and no mistake. Why hadn't the owners castrated the tearaway? "We don't believe in it," they snorted. Well, if ever there was a dog that was crying out for it, this little tyrant was! Tell me what you would prefer, a thug or a lovely family pet? Talk about give a breed a bad name!

★POP STARS OF THE MOMENT★

HERE ARE SOME OF THE POP STARS TO LOOK OUT FOR IN THE NEW MILLENNIUM

Sammy Davis Left Bridge Stewart

The illegitimate son of Dr Who's Brigadier Left Bridge Stewart and Sammy Davis Junior's mum, Sammy Davis Left Bridge Stewart was born in and around Luton, Ohio before hopping on a plane and landing in London airport. Growing up in the London airport branch of Dixons, Sammy soon became familiar with all the latest technology but didn't necessarily know how it worked but was able to read the prices and if he got stuck could go and get the brochure. At the age of sixteen he left Dixons and moved to River Island where he met Jenny, who worked behind the till there. They were married soon after and the birth of their daughter Tilly Sammy Davis Left Bridge Stewart Junior prompted them to seek a larger accommodation in Burger King. His main love is Techno - Clothing music using the sounds of modern technology coupled with the sound that our clothes make when you walk along. First single Corduroy Song (verver ver ver etc.) did not do well but had modest success in the indie clothes market in Wembley. 2,000 looks like a big year for Sammy.

Alfie Broad and the Buttons

Nuffield based Alfie has a BA degree in German and used to work killing people in the war. The war over, Alfie spent some years in Argentina learning the piccolo, taking that special instrument to Grade 8 Seventh Dan. Advised that his look was too old for the current pop markets, Alfie had a series of plastic surgery operations on his face through the seventies and eighties, but his face was always slighty behind the trend. By sticking on one face in 1989 and hoping it would come into fashion Alfie took a gamble, which as the new millennium approaches looks likely to pay off. His debut single, with this particular face anyway, is a cover of "Livin' It Up" by Northern Uproar.

Peeloo

Born Francesca Di Amotto Pancora Del Amitri Ogogogoc in the Isle of Man, "Peeloo" as she has styled herself played her first concert aged nine and released her first disc aged fifteen. Now 53 Peeloo had been honing one song in particular only to find out just three weeks ago that the song - entitled "Where Do You Go To My Lovely" already exists, word for word by Peter Sarstedt. This won't hold Peeloo back and already she is working, polishing up a follow-up single called simply "Mis-Shapes/Sorted For E's And Whizz" which she hopes to have ready by the year 2033.

Penelope Keith Flint

The daughter of Penelope Keith from The Good Life and Keith Flint from The Prodigy, Penny has become renowned as the girl who sings wearing mittens. With hits like "Long Live Living", "Mannequin Of Death" and "Furnishings Of Soil That You Bring And All I Got Was This Lousy Tee Shirt", Penny is difficult to pin down in style. "I just wear my mittens and draw power from them like it's magic or something," she says, showing an insight into her work that belies her Roedean education. Recently signed to the Bratwurst label, the fall should see her new single "The Harvest Is Of Dust And The Furrows Wither Potterton Kingfisher Boiler With Stunning Views Over The Common" hit the very top of the charts.

Jim L. Fixit

The first of the long blond-haired cigar smoking rappers to come out of Derby, Jim has collaborated with Shabba Ranks on his debut single "Now Then Now Then, I Have Here A Letter Which Says Dear Jim". The product of an altogether illegal liaison between Fern Brittan and a hammerhead shark - meant only as a holiday romance. Jim hatched from his capsule and swam the 24,000 miles from the Great Barrier Reef to the River Trent and from thence worked his way overland, in pubs and clubs to Derby. With the advent of CCTV to observe till transactions, Jim fell from favour with the booze trade and with some birthday money bought himself a Yamaha Clavinova PF keyboard and started to strum out his own tunes. After a while he realised that certain words placed next to each other conveyed a meaning to some people and from then on never looked back. Fully self contained, no sole representation.

"A CUT-OUT AND KEEP SAVE 'EM OR SWAP 'EM"

little alan hill

Tap tap tap

radisson

12 · I say Stouff'

may sung

13 · You gimme Abbey National Book!

gareth southgate badger

14 · We're not doing it

mum

15 · Stun Gun!

Johnee Vaughan owl

Ooooh! (thrupppp!)

kenn ford

17 · Hello Harry, love the show

N°s 11-17 in a series of 17 classic trump cards

Barrie Gosney
Flat 4, The Albany
Piccadilly,
London WC1

Bacon

I will not retract a word! You are a low
down filthy coat stealing pig and I have
set the ball rolling to have you expelled
from the club.

Barrie

Gosney

" A ration of lemon juice."

"A CUT-OUT AND KEEP SAVE 'EM OR SWAP 'EM"

Nos 11-17 in a series of 17 classic trump cards

Name:	Gareth Southgate Badger
Age:	30
Job:	Coordinator badger parade
Says:	We're not doing it
Top Speed:	18mph
Hobbies:	Lazing around
Weaknesses:	Kaliber

Name:	May Sung
Age:	40
Job:	Wife and housekeeper to Harry Hill
Says:	You gimme Abbey National book!
Top Speed:	19mph
Hobbies:	Amateur accounting
Weaknesses:	Money

Name:	Radisson
Age:	12
Job:	Hotel Management
Says:	I say Stouff'
Top Speed:	8mph
Hobbies:	Travel
Weaknesses:	Chocolate

Name:	Little Alan Hill
Age:	3
Job:	Schoolboy
Says:	Tap tap tap
Top Speed:	16mph
Hobbies:	Tunnelling
Weaknesses:	Hogan the Harlequin Great Dane

Name:	Kenn Ford
Age:	73
Job:	Life model to The Joy of Sex books
Says:	Hello Harry, love the show
Top Speed:	2mph
Hobbies:	Joy
Weaknesses:	Sex

Name:	Johnee Vaughan Owl
Age:	37
Job:	Presenter Owl
Says:	Oooooh! (thruppp!)
Top Speed:	38mph
Hobbies:	Screenwriting
Weaknesses:	Award ceremonies

Name:	Mum
Age:	Given as 34
Job:	Housewife
Says:	Stun gun!
Top Speed:	17mph
Hobbies:	Recharging stun gun
Weaknesses:	Mark Morrisson

Hilarious Dog Stories
by L. M. Hand
No.5 Ken Rises Above A Misfortune

Ken the *mongrel* was found abandoned on the motorway, yes, you heard me correctly, how can people be so cruel? It beggars belief, doesn't it?

But do you know that dog has bettered himself. "Get the blue ball, Ken!" Can you believe it that *mongrel* can distinguish between colours! "Get the red ball Ken! Not the blue ball, the red ball!" Ken knowingly obliges with the ball of choice and so it goes on. "No, Ken the blue ball..." There is no end to that lovable *mongrel's* performance.

Why not give a home to an abandoned dog?

Gregory Bacon
14 The Strand
London WC1

to Phil Harris
Flat4 Kingsway Mansions
Kingsway
London WC2

Dear Phillip,
I do not know quite what Gosney has been saying but I fear he has fair lost his mind. First he accuses me of stealing his blessed top coat and now your trilby. Please believe me, Phillip, I know nothing of the whereabouts of your head gear, nor for that matter of Gosney's coat. Could we perhaps meet for a drink at the club to discuss this sorry matter?
I do hope you find the hat,
Yours

Gregory Bacon

Greg

Harry's Gardening Tips

1 If rainy - stay in, you can't do gardening if it's wet. (See things to do on a rainy day page 58)

2 If it looks like rain - stay in. The last thing you want is to start and then have to pack everything up again and go indoors as this will knock your confidence. (See page 58).

3 If your dog, like my 4-year-old cocker bitch, is ruining your lawn by fouling, why not just have it slabbed over? This is when the borders between gardening and sweeping become blurred.

4 Silk or plastic flowers are almost as good as the real thing these days and, like conifers and Barbra Streisand, are ageless and evergreen.

5 Get to know your garden's bird life by digging over the soil for 20 mins. - You'll soon find you're a popular fellah! (Don't encourage crows though as technically they are vermin, see pages 58 and 35).

6 Cress is a happy alternative to most garden plants.

7 Don't worry about flies round your bonsai trees, in the scaled down world of the bonsai these are the equivalent of birds.

8 For ideas of types of trellis available, browse round your local garden centre.

9 If you have a problem with kids climbing over the back fence for their ball, plant up what I call a "poison garden" - deadly nightshade, nettles, toadstools, belladonna, poison cap. They'll soon get the message that their ball comes over the fence and now the game is over. It is useful to have a stick to rattle about as well and an air pistol as the last resort.

10 Use household waste as compost but keep back potato peelings - they can be taken along to your local bistro where they'll fry them up and serve them to Sloane Rangers as a starter.

11 If slugs and snails are a problem, set up a natural ecosystem to control them; five frogs will control the slug and snail population in an average sized family garden or yard. A medium sized pig will control the frog population and one young brown bear will control the pig population. You as human being, however, will have to carry out the yearly bear cull.

12 If insects like greenfly or blackfly are a problem, every few months blitz the whole yard with DDT.

Genetically modified
Sild

Britain's most popular oily fish

Now offers protection from SCURF™
In clinical trials those subjects who ate Sild regularly had a 40% decrease in the number of SCURF™ nodules

NEW

GENETICALLY MODIFIED
Sild in Savlon

Available IN OIL IN TOMATO SAUCE or IN SAVLON

SERVING SUGGESTION
Net 110 g ℮

Sild™ - It tastes of fish

ROOKERY BIRD PRODUCTS
Fresh Crow Salami
14 SLICES
SERVING SUGGESTION
70 g ℮

WHILE STOCKS LAST

DISPLAY UNTIL 30 JUN | USE BY 2 JUL
KEEP REFRIGERATED

Fresh Crow
Salami
From Rookery Bird Products

Only the choicest crow pieces have been selected, cured and genetically enhanced with SCURF™ protecting properties. Buy now before Crow is declared officially Vermin.

Also available - Crow off the Bone, Crow Paté and Weird Crow Effigy Thing that you could use in a sort of crow shrine.

Bunty Hoven Letters

Well, we get a lot of letters on the show and here's a few from Bunty Hoven...

Dear Harry,

Over the years there have been many TV stars who have disgraced themselves and betrayed the public and had to duck out of the limelight - however, they still have the skills that put them there in the first place so why not have a TV show just fronted by disgraced TV presenters - "The Shame Show". You could have Frank Bough presenting an item helped by shamed Blue Peter presenter Richard Bacon. Maybe we might just learn to trust them again.

Yours sincerely
Bunty Hoven

Dear Harry,
Basil Brush always went "Ha ha ha ha - Boom! Boom!" after every joke he told. It seems to me a shame that he didn't feel able to rely on the strength of his material to get a laugh, rather than having to signpost every gag with a crude "Boom! Boom!" Where is he now? Yes, I think that proves my point.
Yours Bunty

Dear Harry,
I had to laugh on a recent visit to London. The "townies" now have a shop called "Naff-Naff", another called "Hyper-hyper" and another called "The Carphone Warehouse". Don't they realise that's exactly what London is - a naff, hyper place for phonies!
Yours Bunty
PS Bentalls is good too.

Dear Harry

I imagine living under a communist regime is a bit like one of those proud shops where everything is a pound - only it's not a pound due to rampant inflation - a by product of the harsh communists regime of "full" employment. Hundred pound shops more like!
Up the Workers
Yours

"Comrade" Bunty

Dear Harry,
By moving News at Ten to the earlier slot of 6.30 Trevor might find that not enough has happened by 6.30 to fill a whole half hour but we don't want you just making stories up, Trevor. How about a news programme that just deals with positive news stories - a kind of "News Lite" for pensioners and the infirm - cats being rescued, people getting better for a change. Come on ITV!
Yours Bunty

Dear Harry,
At Princess Diana's funeral Elton John sang "It seems to me that you lived your life like a candle in the wind", well, as regards HM The Queen Mum - at 99 years of age it seems to me that she has "lived her life like an oxyacetylene tool in a virtually no-breeze situation".
There's one for you, Mr John!
Bunty

Dear Harry,
If global warming takes place and the polar ice caps melt, who's going to look after 15 million homeless eskimos? I'm not having one I'll tell you that.

Yours sincerely
Bunty Hoven
PS, Oh we'll have no problem placing Bjork, but what about the rest of them

---

Dear Harry,
Remember Live Aid back in 1985? It had over 60 million viewers but still didn't get a series. What have our young entertainers got to do to get on TV these days?
Yours Bunty

Dear Harry,
JMW Turner, the well known painter, is famous for his sunsets but did he paint them because he liked sunsets or because he could get cheap orange paint?
Think on it
Bunty

Jill Gosney-Peters
"Sampfire"
Chalfont St. Giles
Bucks

Dear Barrie,

Just returned from Minorca to find your letter. You never had a grey coat you chump! The coat I bought you from Simpsons was a green top coat. Are you covered under your household insurance? I have the receipt somewhere if you are to make a claim.

The holiday was wonderful and we're thoroughly rested. Love to Jaquii,

Jill

Dear Harry
The use by date on my Ardennes Paté says it should be used within three days of purchase. Does this still apply as I use it as a powerful adhesive!
Love to all,
Bunty

May Sung

Kenn Ford

GUIDE   HOW TO TELL IF YOUR FOOD IS STALE

There are numbers printed on the lids of many foods that can help you work out whether your food is off or o.k.

eg 1.
YOGHURT

Take these 3 numbers and add them together

15
+ 4
+ 99
TOTAL A: 118

Look at your video recorder

Add these numbers together

12
+ 2
99
TOTAL B 113

If Total B is small less than total A the food is safe to eat !!

Names you won't ever see down a stick of rock!

IT COULD NEVER HAPPEN!

Crossword (p57)

(p57)

Across/down answers visible in grid:

- GOOD
- ANNE MCINTOSH
- DUNCAN
- WIDE
- POND
- THEATRE
- HIT IN THE 90S
- CLARE
- GREASEPAINT
- PRISON
- A FORGE
- THE ANSWER
- AS A CHET (ASACHET)
- BIRDS
- BONNIE LANGFORDS LEGS
- MONKHOUSE

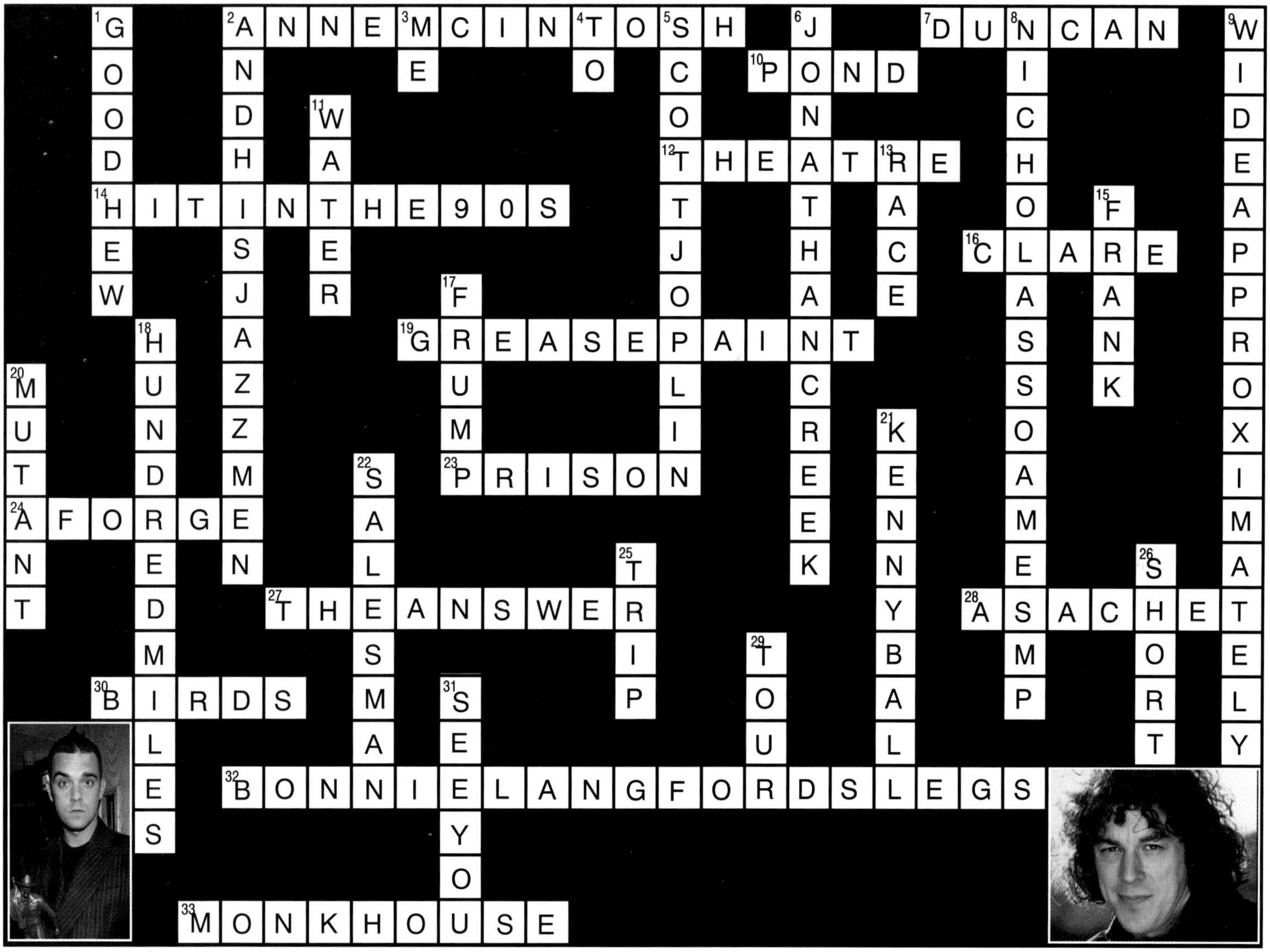

Jigsaw Faces (p53)

Answers: 1. Shimon Perez 2. Anwar Sadat 3. Benjamin Netenyahu 4. Sally Chipperfield
5. Jacqueline Bouvier Kennedy Onassis 5. Vanessa Feltz

(p53)

Other Books by Harry Hill

If you've enjoyed reading this book you might be interested in these other titles by Harry Hill
Let 'em Scream - Surviving parenthood · **Just Fry It!** - Common sense cookery
Don't Let Them Breed - Charles and Camilla, a love story
Didn't You See The Sticker? - Your guide to not paying in bob-a-job week · **Fill It Paint It Flog It** - A guide to selling your car
It's Supposed To Make That Noise - Advanced car selling · **My Face Hurts - Can I Stop Smiling Now?** - Blair's Britain
Wait A Minute, If I'm The Son Of Man, What Am I Doing Up Here? - The Bible explained

Other Books by Boxtree Publishing

The Priory Cookbook - What The Stars Eat When They're Freakin' Out by Barzden Meades
How To Make Your Face Into A Badge by Vanessa Feltz · **The Rough Guide To SCURF™** by Trevor Hess
Papier Mâché As Make-Up by Barbara Cartland · **Pork Bagel** by The Naughty But Nice Jewish Cook Book

INDEX

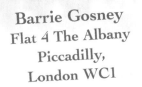

Barrie Gosney
Flat 4 The Albany
Piccadilly,
London WC1

Dear Greg,

What a chump I've been! I received a
communication from Jill in response to my letter
of some three weeks ago, upon her return from
holidaying in Minorca - It seems I did not ever
have a grey coat - rather a green coat- which
has been hanging in my wardrobe all this time!
For some reason I took it into my head that I
had worn a grey coat to the club that night and
when I could not find it I assumed it to be
lost. I fear I may even have suggested that you
were in someway involved in its disappearance.
Let me reassure you now that I have the green
coat - and the "Dents" gloves and other items
in its pockets, safe and sound with me at my
rooms and apologise profusely for any
misunderstanding that may have arisen out of
this slight faux pas.
Will you join me for a drink at the Club
Tuesday week?
Your friend

Barrie
x x

Barrie
cc Phil Harris, Sir Arthur Pimm, Arthur Bootle

THANKS TO

MAGDA ARCHER

JAMIE ACOTT & NICK LINFORD

PETER QUINNELL

RICHARD ALLEN-TURNER
JON THODAY & ED THOMSON

CLARE HULTON
& ADRIAN SINGTON

BURT KWOUK

AL MURRAY

MATT BRADSTOCK

BARRIE GOSNEY

SHEILA DUNN

HÉLÉNE PATAROT

DR. M.K. HALL

KITTY, WINNIE & HATTIE HALL

REMEMBER: your book may go up as well as down.